Kingdom
of the Dead

P E T E R   A C K R O Y D

LONDON, NEW YORK, MUNICH, MELBOURNE, and DELHI

Senior editor David John
Editor Susan Kennedy
Senior art editor Stefan Podhorodecki
Project art editors Joe Conneally,
Philip Letsu, Floyd Sayers
Managing editor Andrew Macintyre
Managing art editor Jane Thomas
Publishing manager Caroline Buckingham
Publishing director Jonathan Metcalf
Production controller Rochelle Talary
DTP designer Siu Yin Ho
Picture researchers Jo de Gray, Sarah Pownall
Picture librarians Sarah Mills, Karl Stange
Jacket designer Neal Cobourne

Consultant
James Putnam

First American Edition, 2004

Published in the United States by
DK Publishing, Inc.
375 Hudson Street
New York, New York 10014

04 05 06 07 08 10 9 8 7 6 5 4 3 2 1

A Cataloging-in-Publication record for this book
is available from the Library of Congress.

ISBN 0-7566-0846-5

Reproduced by Media, Development and Printing Ltd.
Printed and bound in Italy by L.E.G.O.

Discover more at
www.dk.com

Contents

In the beginning was water and darkness. Out of this water, this original ocean called "nun," emerged the creator god, Atum.

The god took the form of a heron that perched upon a mound in the middle of the water. There, he gave a great cry, and this first sound began the process of creation. Darkness shared existence with light, and the unknown became known. In a temple at Heliopolis, "the City of the Sun," in ancient Egypt, the rock upon which Atum perched was worshiped. It had become a sacred stone in the form of a small pyramid covered with gold.

The Egyptians had other myths of creation, all of them linked with the sun and with water. A wading bird known as an ibis, the embodiment of the god Thoth, laid an egg upon the mound, and from this egg creation was born. Or perhaps a lotus flower emerged upon the surface of the waters of darkness; when it unfurled its petals, the sun god, Ra, stepped from it in the form of a boy.

For the Egyptians, whether priest or peasant, king or shepherd, all these stories were true. The stories explained the world as the Egyptians knew it. Their lives were dominated by the heat and light of the sun. They relied upon the waters of the Nile to give them life. But the sun gave way to darkness every evening and, as we will see, the waters of the Nile only rose in flood once every year. Light and darkness were part of the same cycle. The rising and setting of the sun made it clear that creation must happen again every day.

The Egyptians believed that Nut, the goddess of the sky, swallowed the sun every evening. The sun passed into the underworld until Nut gave birth to it again each morning. That is why the dead were believed to come alive in the underworld. Rebirth followed death, just as the Nile receded and then returned.

As Ra said, "When I cried, man was created in the form of tears flowing from my eyes." Life and water were intimately connected, even when water took the form of sadness. The Egyptians believed that Egypt was at the center of the universe. Beyond its frontiers lay hostility and chaos. In their myths of creation, the island of origin is floating upon an ocean of dark waters. The fertile ground of Egypt was also surrounded by the desert wastes, and this boundary between life and death affected all of their beliefs. Just as the sun marked the circuit of life from east to west, so the Nile River marked its life from south to north. The Nile was at the center of everything Egyptian. It was the country's source of food. It was the country's nurse and mother. It was the water from which creation came.

CHAPTER ONE

The lord of the two lands

In the summer of every year, in July and August, the Nile River would rise in flood and break its banks. To those who were not Egyptian, this was a most extraordinary and baffling event. It seemed to be contrary to nature.

THE GREEK HISTORIAN Herodotus wrote, "I could get no information, from the priests or from anyone, about the reasons for the behavior of the Nile." Without an explanation for this miraculous rebirth of the water every year, in the hottest and driest months, the ancient Egyptians naturally believed it to be an event

determined by the gods. We know now that the Nile has its source far to the south of Egypt at Lake Victoria, in modern Uganda, and that it is swollen by summer rains in Ethiopia before sweeping through Sudan and Egypt on its way to the Mediterranean Sea. When the waters reached the narrow Nile Valley in Egypt, they overflowed the riverbanks and flooded the land.

The effects of the annual flood on Egypt were profound. The waters brought such fertility to the land that even in the earliest times, Egypt had a prosperous and even

◀ The Nile near Thebes (modern Luxor)

CYCLE OF LIFE
Without the fertility of the riverbanks, there would have been no civilization in Egypt. Farming revolved around the annual flood until 1971, when a dam built at Aswan changed the behavior of the Nile.

NILE ANIMALS
The Nile teemed with life. Men caught many types of fish with nets or hooks and lines. Children were taught to be afraid of crocodiles and hippos, which could overturn papyrus boats.

luxurious civilization. Every year, the river left a rich deposit of black mud on the fields beside the river. This mud, rich in nutrients, was perfect for growing cereals such as wheat and barley. After the waters had fallen in October and November, the Egyptian farmers sowed their grain in the fresh mud and harvested an abundant crop in the following spring. The cycle then began again when the Nile flooded a few months later. Each year the Nile rose, and each year was a new beginning.

The ancient Egyptians called their country *Kemet*, the Black Land, after this fertile strip of rich, dark soil along either bank of the Nile. That is why the Egyptians thought of black as a lucky color. Here was the luxuriant plant life of Egypt—the pomegranate trees and the grapevines, the onions and the figs. Here, animals grazed—the sheep and the pigs, the antelopes and the gazelles. In the river itself there lived hippos and crocodiles, while papyrus reeds grew in the marshlands.

The Black Land was the opposite of the Red Land or *Deshret*, from which our own word "desert" springs. This Red Land was one of the driest regions on Earth. The Black Land was life, and the Red Land was dryness, famine, and death.

And so the Nile was of crucial importance to the Egyptians. Their calendar was based on it. The Dog Star, Sirius, which the Egyptians

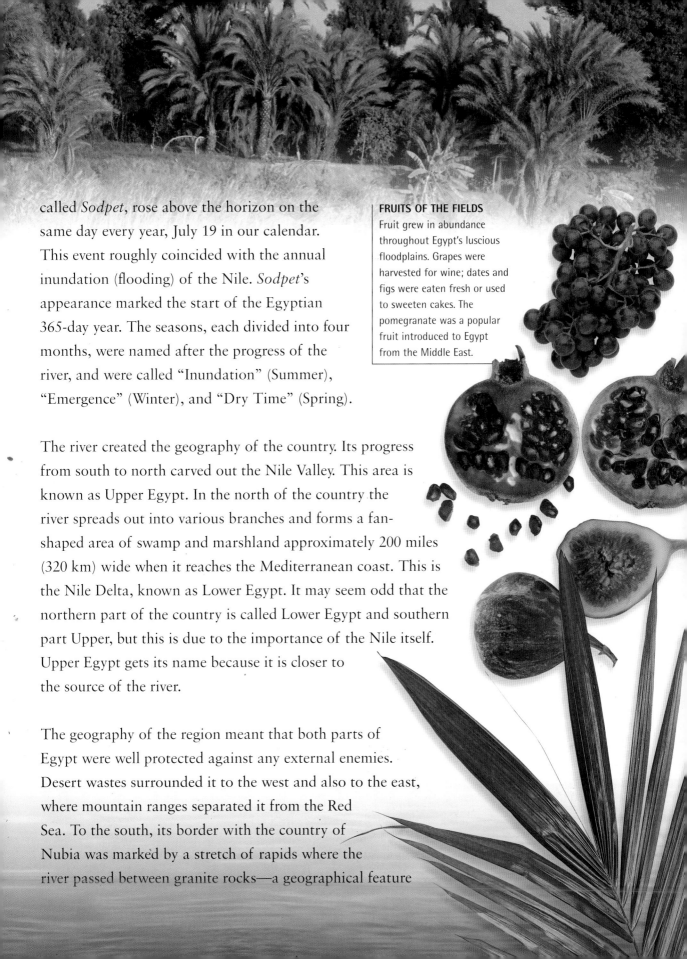

called *Sodpet*, rose above the horizon on the same day every year, July 19 in our calendar. This event roughly coincided with the annual inundation (flooding) of the Nile. *Sodpet*'s appearance marked the start of the Egyptian 365-day year. The seasons, each divided into four months, were named after the progress of the river, and were called "Inundation" (Summer), "Emergence" (Winter), and "Dry Time" (Spring).

The river created the geography of the country. Its progress from south to north carved out the Nile Valley. This area is known as Upper Egypt. In the north of the country the river spreads out into various branches and forms a fan-shaped area of swamp and marshland approximately 200 miles (320 km) wide when it reaches the Mediterranean coast. This is the Nile Delta, known as Lower Egypt. It may seem odd that the northern part of the country is called Lower Egypt and southern part Upper, but this is due to the importance of the Nile itself. Upper Egypt gets its name because it is closer to the source of the river.

The geography of the region meant that both parts of Egypt were well protected against any external enemies. Desert wastes surrounded it to the west and also to the east, where mountain ranges separated it from the Red Sea. To the south, its border with the country of Nubia was marked by a stretch of rapids where the river passed between granite rocks—a geographical feature

FRUITS OF THE FIELDS

Fruit grew in abundance throughout Egypt's luscious floodplains. Grapes were harvested for wine; dates and figs were eaten fresh or used to sweeten cakes. The pomegranate was a popular fruit introduced to Egypt from the Middle East.

known as the first cataract. The Mediterranean Sea was Egypt's northern border. This isolation from the rest of the world may explain why, in their mythology, the Egyptians believed themselves to be at the center of the universe.

From very early times people settled in the Nile Valley. When humans first inhabited the region, the climate and the terrain were quite different. The desert had not taken hold of North Africa, and there were lakes where now there is only the sand of the Western Desert. But between 7,000 and 6,000 years ago, the climate grew warmer. The lakes of the Western Desert dried up and the people moved to live beside the great river. They fished from boats, hunted animals, grew crops, and built houses of mud and straw. Gradually, these Nile dwellers traveled northward until they reached the edge of the Nile Delta. Historians know them as the Naqada Culture.

The people of the Naqada Culture buried their dead with grave goods such as jewelry and spoons, pots and flint knives, ebony combs and copper beads. In time, more than 5,000 years ago, the Naqada's descendants came to be ruled by kings who are shown in carvings with beards in the shape of a triangle. Statues of the later Egyptian pharaohs often show them wearing a similar ritual beard. There is a genuine continuity here, which suggests that the civilization of Egypt emerged not out of nowhere, but from these early Nile settlers.

PARADISE LOST
The once-fertile plains of the Sahara supported tribes of hunter-gatherers. When the Sahara became desert, the tribes settled in the Nile Valley.

GEOGRAPHY AND CIVILIZATION

Egypt's isolation and unique geography can be seen in this
satellite image. The Nile Valley gave rise to a civilization that
was closed off from the rest of the world by deserts and sea.

Great changes had taken place in Egypt by
about 3400 BCE. Within a fairly short period
of time, the country's various tribal cultures
evolved into two separate monarchies. The
king of Upper Egypt (the Nile Valley) wore
the White Crown, and the king of Lower Egypt
(the Delta) wore the Red Crown. The symbols
of Upper Egypt were the lotus flower and the
vulture, while those of Lower Egypt were the
papyrus reed and the cobra. The vulture goddess
and the cobra goddess were enemies, until eventually
they were united in the Egypt of the pharaohs.

These mysterious early kings were celebrated in carvings
on ceremonial clubs called mace-heads—important objects
that symbolized the king's authority. One such mace-head
shows a figure wearing the White Crown of Upper Egypt
with a scorpion before his face. Historians have given him
the name King Scorpion and believe he was one of the kings
who slowly conquered the northern regions of the country

LOTUS FLOWERS AND PAPYRUS REEDS

These emblems were favorite decorative devices in
Egypt. Pillars were carved to resemble papyrus bundles,
and colorful lotus-flower tiles adorned the palaces.

GOD OF LIGHT AND LIFE
Horus was one of Egypt's principal gods. He was the hawk god high in the sky whose eyes were the sun and the moon.

in the period before the two lands of Upper and Lower Egypt were unified under one ruler. Archaeologists discovered the King Scorpion mace-head in the ruins of the temple of Horus in the town of Hieraconpolis, one of the oldest sites in Egypt. Horus was the god of light and life. He was the falcon-headed god who controlled the skies and who became the guardian of Egypt itself. The pharaohs were

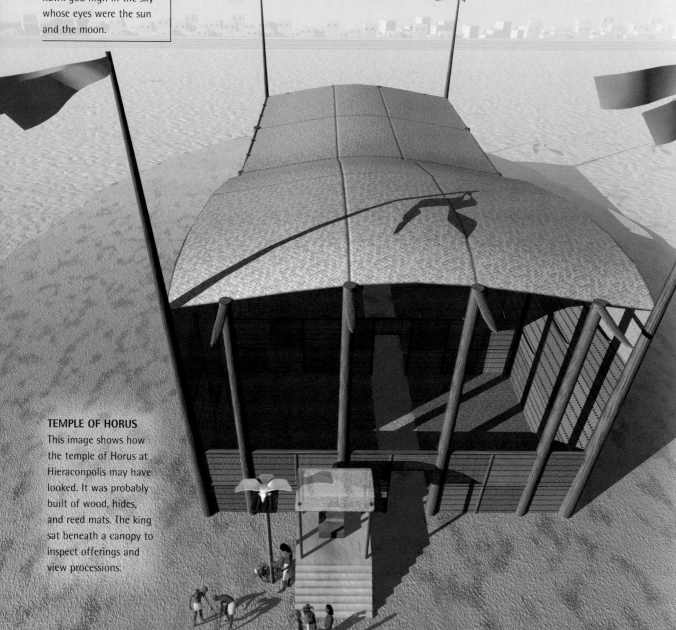

TEMPLE OF HORUS
This image shows how the temple of Horus at Hieraconpolis may have looked. It was probably built of wood, hides, and reed mats. The king sat beneath a canopy to inspect offerings and view processions.

thought to be his living embodiment on earth. Clearly, then, some of the gods of Egypt emerged at a very early date indeed.

ROYAL CLUB
Upper Egypt's triumph over the Delta is recorded on the Narmer Palette. Here, King Narmer wears the White Crown as he clubs his enemy's head. This posture became a symbol of royal power in Egypt.

The most famous of the early kings is Narmer, who made himself king of both Upper and Lower Egypt in about 3100 BCE. An object known as the Narmer Palette, an elaborately carved stone slab, shows him on one side wearing the Red Crown of Lower Egypt and on the other the White Crown of Upper Egypt. Two hieroglyphs (picture symbols), one of a catfish, "nar," and the other of a chisel, "mer," spell out his name, Narmer. One scene on the Palette depicts him as a bull demolishing a walled town, a powerful image that may represent Narmer's conquest of the northern people of the Delta. On the other side, he is raising his mace to strike a prisoner whom he is grasping by the hair.

RED KING
On the Palette's reverse side, Narmer, in the Red Crown, inspects the bound and beheaded bodies of his prisoners.

From the achievements of these early kings emerged the first pharaoh of what is known as the First Dynasty (a word that simply means "family"). He was called Menes, although some historians believe that Narmer and Menes were one and the same person. The word "pharaoh" comes from the ancient Egyptian *per'aa*, or "great house," meaning the palace where the king lived. Over time, the sense of the word changed, until it came to refer to the king himself.

The pharaohs who followed Menes stretch in a long line from the First Dynasty, founded in about 3100 BCE, to the 30th Dynasty, which came to an end in 343 BCE, a period of nearly 3,000 years. From first to last there were about 170 pharaohs, and most of them ruled with enormous power.

Menes founded a new capital city for the unified state of Egypt, which was known as White Walls because the limestone walls that surrounded the royal palace gleamed in the hot sun. They also gave it a name meaning "the Balance of the Two Lands" (Upper and Lower Egypt). We know it as Memphis, the name the Greeks gave it. It remained one of the principal cities of Egypt for 3,000 years.

Menes reigned for 62 years and is said to have been killed and eaten by a hippopotamus, no doubt while on a hunt. However, with events as remote in time as these, it is sometimes difficult to tell where legend ends and history begins. We do know that Menes was buried in a vast royal cemetery at Abydos in the middle part of Egypt. It seems that several members of his household were killed at the time of his funeral and buried

Art from stone and gold

From the earliest dynasties, Egyptians were carving with more than 40 types of stone, among them quartzite and sandstone, limestone and diorite, and red and black granite from quarries in the deserts. Gold was another favorite substance of permanence. The eastern desert between the Nile and the Red Sea was rich in gold-bearing rock, which the Egyptians mined from early in their history.

Red quartzite head of Djedefra, Fourth Dynasty

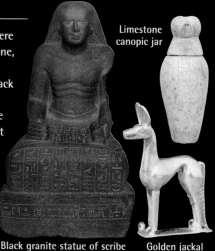

Limestone canopic jar

Black granite statue of scribe

Golden jackal

with him, perhaps to serve him in the afterlife.
Abydos contains many other royal tombs. When
a tomb from the First Dynasty was opened at the
beginning of the 20th century, the perfume of the
aromatic oils used to anoint the body 5,000 years
earlier still hung in the air.

The First and Second Dynasty kings ruled Egypt
for more than 500 years until about 2686 BCE, but
historians have only patchy knowledge of their names
and deeds, gathered from a few scattered inscriptions
and the evidence of ritual burials. Dynasties change
from one to the next when a pharaoh dies without
leaving an heir or when another family seizes power.
The last pharaoh of the Second Dynasty,
Khasekhemwy, built a vast burial chamber at
Abydos. This was one of the earliest structures
in Egypt and a sign of what was to come in the
monumental use of stone.

Throughout their history, the ancient Egyptians
expressed themselves in vast creations of stone,
whether in statues or temples or pyramids.
To the Egyptians, stone may have suggested
greatness and permanence in the shifting
desert landscape of sand and dunes.
They built their houses and shops, even
their royal palaces, out of wood or mud
bricks, which do not last. That was
because ordinary human life was
considered to be perishable; everlasting
life came after death. Tombs, therefore,

This statue of the Second
Dynasty king Khasekhemwy
shows that Egypt's formal
artistic style was already
established in this very
early period. The eyes
are fixed straight
ahead, while the
arms and feet are
rigidly stylized.

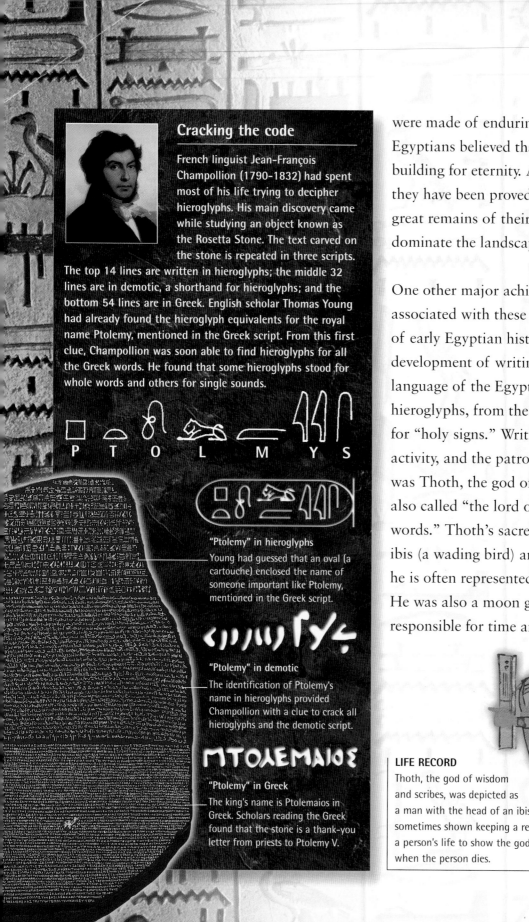

Cracking the code

French linguist Jean-François Champollion (1790-1832) had spent most of his life trying to decipher hieroglyphs. His main discovery came while studying an object known as the Rosetta Stone. The text carved on the stone is repeated in three scripts. The top 14 lines are written in hieroglyphs; the middle 32 lines are in demotic, a shorthand for hieroglyphs; and the bottom 54 lines are in Greek. English scholar Thomas Young had already found the hieroglyph equivalents for the royal name Ptolemy, mentioned in the Greek script. From this first clue, Champollion was soon able to find hieroglyphs for all the Greek words. He found that some hieroglyphs stood for whole words and others for single sounds.

P T O L M Y S

"Ptolemy" in hieroglyphs
Young had guessed that an oval (a cartouche) enclosed the name of someone important like Ptolemy, mentioned in the Greek script.

"Ptolemy" in demotic
The identification of Ptolemy's name in hieroglyphs provided Champollion with a clue to crack all hieroglyphs and the demotic script.

ΠΤΟΛΕΜΑΙΟΣ

"Ptolemy" in Greek
The king's name is Ptolemaios in Greek. Scholars reading the Greek found that the stone is a thank-you letter from priests to Ptolemy V.

were made of enduring stone. The Egyptians believed that they were building for eternity. And, in that belief, they have been proved right. The great remains of their civilization still dominate the landscape of the country.

One other major achievement is associated with these obscure passages of early Egyptian history: the development of writing. The written language of the Egyptians is called hieroglyphs, from the Greek word for "holy signs." Writing was a sacred activity, and the patron god of writing was Thoth, the god of wisdom, who was also called "the lord of the divine words." Thoth's sacred animals were the ibis (a wading bird) and the baboon, and he is often represented in these forms. He was also a moon god, and was responsible for time and for counting.

LIFE RECORD
Thoth, the god of wisdom and scribes, was depicted as a man with the head of an ibis. He is sometimes shown keeping a record of a person's life to show the gods when the person dies.

He had many duties, therefore, and remained one of the principal gods of Egypt throughout its history.

The invention of writing probably predates the unification of Egypt under the early kings, and its first use was to list goods and the names of officials. In that sense, writing developed as an instrument of power. It was crucial in creating a government and a state. The Narmer Palette shows us that hieroglyphs were used at an early date to identify rulers in royal art and in tombs. It was a way of confirming their power and their sacredness. Writing helped to create a state religion, and it had power over death as well as over life. Hieroglyphs created what have become known as the "Pyramid Texts," magic written on the walls of tombs to help the deceased in the journey through the underworld.

The Egyptians left behind a vast treasury of writings— religious texts, histories, business letters, stories. But when the age of the pharaohs ended some 2,000 years ago, the use of hieroglyphs was forgotten. Visitors to Egypt marveled at the relics of a vanished civilization but understood little about it because no one could read the writing. Hieroglyphs remained a secret until 1822, when they were finally decoded by the French linguist Jean-François Champollion. Thanks to his great discovery, scholars known as Egyptologists could learn about the world of the Egyptians and hear voices from the ancient past speaking again.

WRITING HIEROGLYPHS
Hieroglyphs could be written from left to right, right to left, or from top to bottom, like these. For everyday writing, scribes used faster-written versions called hieratic and, later, demotic.

CHAPTER TWO

The *pyramid* age

About 4,500 years ago, Egypt came under the rule of the Third Dynasty kings. It was the start of a 500-year golden period of stability and prosperity in Egypt's history, known as the Old Kingdom. It was also the dawn of the Pyramid Age.

THE DYNASTY'S SECOND PHARAOH, DJOSER, changed the face of Egypt forever. Although he reigned for only 19 years, Egyptians still celebrated his memory more than 2,500 years after his death. And what was the reason for this extraordinary fame? Djoser built the first pyramid. Djoser's pyramid, the first truly monumental stone building in the world, stood in the desert region of Saqqara, close to Memphis. It was a step pyramid rather than a smooth-sided pyramid, and was built of six huge steps of stone, placed one above the other, to a height of more than 200 ft (60 m). The steps were covered with white limestone that would have gleamed and glittered in the intense desert sun. The bottom step measured about 350 ft by 400 ft (106 m by

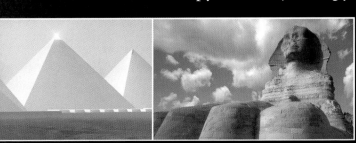

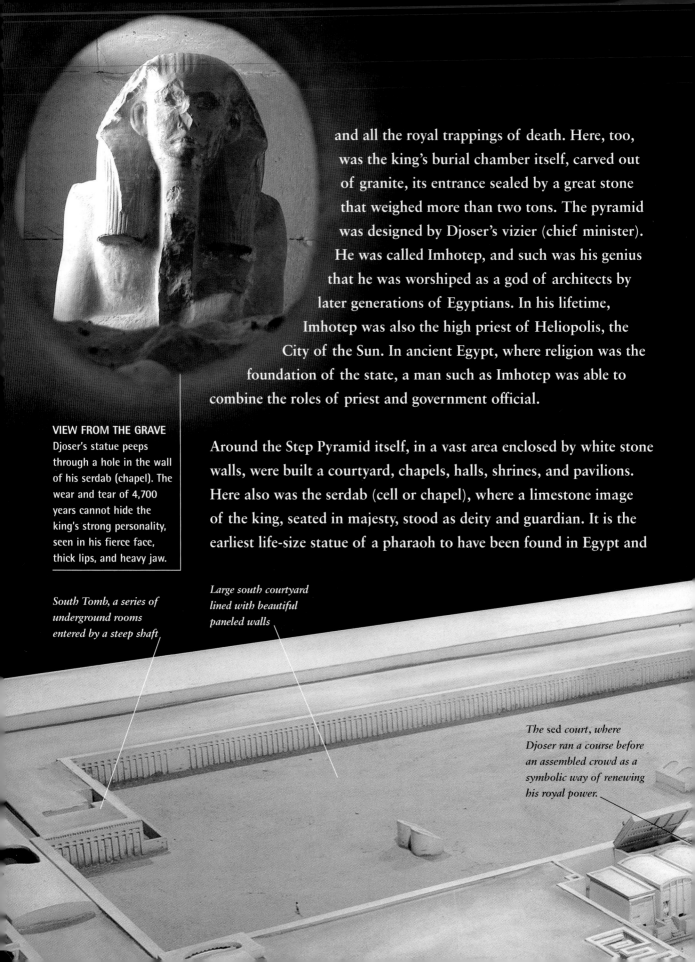

and all the royal trappings of death. Here, too, was the king's burial chamber itself, carved out of granite, its entrance sealed by a great stone that weighed more than two tons. The pyramid was designed by Djoser's vizier (chief minister). He was called Imhotep, and such was his genius that he was worshiped as a god of architects by later generations of Egyptians. In his lifetime, Imhotep was also the high priest of Heliopolis, the City of the Sun. In ancient Egypt, where religion was the foundation of the state, a man such as Imhotep was able to combine the roles of priest and government official.

Around the Step Pyramid itself, in a vast area enclosed by white stone walls, were built a courtyard, chapels, halls, shrines, and pavilions. Here also was the serdab (cell or chapel), where a limestone image of the king, seated in majesty, stood as deity and guardian. It is the earliest life-size statue of a pharaoh to have been found in Egypt and

VIEW FROM THE GRAVE
Djoser's statue peeps through a hole in the wall of his serdab (chapel). The wear and tear of 4,700 years cannot hide the king's strong personality, seen in his fierce face, thick lips, and heavy jaw.

South Tomb, a series of underground rooms entered by a steep shaft

Large south courtyard lined with beautiful paneled walls

The sed court, where Djoser ran a course before an assembled crowd as a symbolic way of renewing his royal power.

has the mystery of an original creations. Through two small holes bored in the wall of the serdab, the eyes of Djoser's statue could "see" out into the world and watch the priests leave the offerings that nourished him in the afterlife. This complex of buildings was intended as a palace where the king could rule after his death and continue to perform all the rituals that kept the world in order. The Step Pyramid, and the buildings that surrounded it, were a symbol of the pharaoh's lasting power, even from beyond the grave.

To Egyptians, the pharaoh was a god. Djoser's amazing building achievement must have helped to enforce this idea in the Egyptian mind. The pharaoh was thought to be filled with the divine power of

ROYAL RUN
A chamber beneath the South Tomb is carved with this commemoration of Djoser's *sed* festival. The king was required to run a course in the *sed* court to prove his fitness to rule.

STEP PYRAMID COMPLEX
The Step Pyramid is part of a large complex of ritual buildings. However, many of the buildings are dummies, and many of the doors are fakes that do not open. These may have had a magical meaning.

Under the pyramid lies a vast network of passages, and the king's burial chamber.

The body of the pyramid is made of small stone blocks laid like bricks.

Dummy chapels

Red Crown

Crook

Cobra head

Ritual beard

Nemes
headdress

Flail

the falcon-headed god Horus, and, at a later date, to be the offspring of the sun god, Ra, himself. After his death, the pharaoh became "as one with" Osiris, the king of the dead.

The pharaoh was, in all essentials, the king of the world. He was both human and divine. He maintained the balance of the seasons and assured the harmonious movement of the stars; he was responsible for the annual flooding of the Nile, and protected his country from the forces of chaos that were ranged against it. He defended Egypt against poverty, famine, and conquest. He guaranteed the rising of the sun and oversaw the cycle of life, death, and rebirth. He celebrated the rituals that connected the living and the

The symbols of the pharaoh

In images, the pharaoh holds a shepherd's crook and a flail (a tool for threshing wheat) in his hands. The crook represents kingship and the flail the fertility of the land. Sometimes he carries an ankh, an object shaped like a small, looped cross. The ankh was a symbol of life itself, and was worn for good luck. The pharaoh often wore a cobra made of gold as part of his headdress, and a ceremonial false beard tied to his chin. He had a broad collar of gold, and a bull's tail hung from his waist as another symbol of his power. On state occasions, he wore the double crown of Egypt that combined the White Crown and the Red Crown of the two lands.

The pharaoh's names

Pharaohs were given up to five separate names. One was the "Horus name" he took when he was crowned—for example, "He who unites the Two Lands." The last, which was always shown inside a type of oval called a cartouche (*right*), was his birth name, which is the name we know him by today. The names of very early pharaohs were written inside a box called a serekh (*left*).

Serekh

Cartouche

PYRAMID PROGRESS
Building techniques were advancing rapidly by the Fourth Dynasty. Sneferu's Bent Pyramid is made from huge slabs, unlike the small blocks of the Step Pyramid.

dead and was the bridge between the human world and the divine world. One Egyptian text says that the pharaoh "is the realization of that which is in hearts, his eyes look through all bodies. He is the sun god under whose leadership man lives… He is the sun god through whose rays man sees." So the pharaoh represented supreme power. He was perfect. He was never wrong. Images of him, whether in paint or in stone, depict him with a calm and unworried gaze; he looks beyond human time at eternity.

Djoser's pyramid started a trend, and for the next 800 years many of Egypt's rulers built pyramids throughout the land. At first, the pharaohs continued to build step pyramids like Djoser's. Then Sneferu, the founder of the Fourth Dynasty (2613–2498 BCE), experimented with a new shape. He began with a step pyramid, perhaps built by an earlier king, and packed stones around the steps. He then cased the whole structure in limestone blocks. Sneferu had created the first smooth-sided pyramid, known today as the Meidum Pyramid. Another of Sneferu's pyramids is the "Bent Pyramid." The builders started building its sides at a very steep pitch but changed the angle of slope halfway through its construction, probably because cracks began to appear. The "Red Pyramid," named after the color of the stone when lit by the evening sun, is thought to be Sneferu's actual burial place, though his body vanished long ago.

MIGHTY SNEFERU
Sneferu holds the record for pyramid-building. He built no less than three during his 24-year reign, two for himself and one for his predecessor. Sneferu was an ambitious pharaoh who won wars in Libya and built many new temples, fortresses, and palaces.

THE CRUELTY OF KHUFU
This tiny sculpture is one of only two images ever found of Khufu, builder of the Great Pyramid. Greek historians later described him as a wicked king who forced the whole country to work on his tomb. His stern face can be seen even on this miniature.

Khufu, Sneferu's son and successor, seems to have deliberately competed with his father's achievements by building the biggest pyramid in the world. The Great Pyramid, as it is known, was built on a foundation of solid rock on a plateau named Giza, and rose to a height of 480 ft (146 m). No building rivaled it in height until the 19th century, almost 4,000 years after its construction. Even today, it remains the largest stone building in the world.

The ancient Greeks and Romans considered Khufu's Great Pyramid to be one of the Seven Wonders of the Ancient World, and it is the only one of those wonders that remains today. But in a sense its heart is gone. Khufu was buried within the pyramid itself, rather than in an underground chamber. His sarcophagus, carved out of one huge block of red granite, still remains, but its contents were stolen long ago.

Perhaps the king made use of the great ship discovered by archaeologists buried in the sand next to the pyramid. More than 130 ft (40 m) long and carved out of cedar wood, it was probably used to carry his

THE GREAT PYRAMID
Until the Eiffel Tower opened in 1887, the Great Pyramid was the tallest structure in the world. This 4,500-year-old mountain of stone contains almost 2.3 million blocks. Its top 33 ft (10 m) and all of its smooth limestone casing were stripped long ago to build medieval Cairo.

body to its burial place. Workmen then took it apart into more than 650 pieces and placed them within the pyramid complex so that the king would have a boat in which to sail across the heavens.

There are the remains of about 90 pyramids in Egypt. The geometry of their shape was clearly important to the Egyptians. The Egyptian name for pyramid is *mur*, which means "place of ascension," and it seems the shape somehow enabled the pharaoh's soul to ascend to the stars. The modern name comes from the Greek word *pyramis*, which was a triangular cake made out of wheat—a very much more ordinary description for the pyramids' distinctive shape.

Inside the Great Pyramid

The Great Pyramid is riddled with shafts, tunnels, and chambers. Khufu's burial chamber is approached through the so-called Grand Gallery, which may have been used to park the giant blocks that once sealed the pyramid. Strange shafts leading from the pyramid's chambers may have been built to allow Khufu's soul to travel to the stars. In 1993, a small robot sent up one of the shafts reached a sealed stone door, raising the possibility that more chambers remain to be discovered.

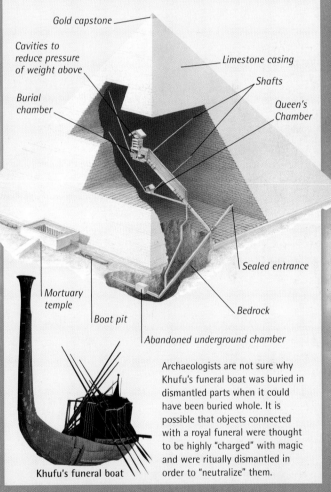

Gold capstone

Cavities to reduce pressure of weight above

Limestone casing

Shafts

Burial chamber

Queen's Chamber

Sealed entrance

Mortuary temple

Boat pit

Bedrock

Abandoned underground chamber

Khufu's funeral boat

Archaeologists are not sure why Khufu's funeral boat was buried in dismantled parts when it could have been buried whole. It is possible that objects connected with a royal funeral were thought to be highly "charged" with magic and were ritually dismantled in order to "neutralize" them.

ROUTE TO STARDOM

Narrow shafts leading from the King's Chamber, deep inside the Great Pyramid, point toward the North Star and the constellation Orion (*right*). Egyptologists are divided about whether the pyramids were portals for sending the pharaoh to join the sun god, Ra, or to join Orion as an "unsetting star." The enigmatic spells of the Pyramid Texts mention both.

But why were the pyramids ever built? Their obvious purpose was to safeguard the body of the pharaoh. It was his last resting place, and the site of his rebirth in the afterlife. But the pyramids were not simply great tombs. They dominate the landscape on which they are set. They are lighthouses in the desert wastes. They suggest mightiness and magnitude. They celebrate the grandeur of the pharaoh.

The pharaohs built their pyramids at various sites along the edge of the desert on the west side of the Nile Valley, where the entrance to the underworld was thought to lie. The pyramids were angled east–west in line with the daily rising of the sun. In other words, the pyramids were part of the cult of the sun that took hold in Egypt at this time. Even the pyramids' shape symbolized this solar worship. Sloping sides radiate out from a central point—the capstone—like beams of light from the sun itself. The capstone may even have been covered with a sheet of gold. Just imagine the sight as the dawn's first rays caught the tips of

THE PYRAMIDS OF GIZA

The Giza pyramids were built with amazing geometrical accuracy. The four sides of each are aligned almost exactly with true north, south, east, and west. We can only guess at what magical meaning this had for the builders. This reconstruction shows how the pyramids may have looked at the end of the Fourth Dynasty, in about 2500 BCE.

these vast monuments, and shone out over the desert. When they were newly completed, and finished off in smooth white limestone, it must have seemed as though the gods themselves had made them.

The pyramids are also proof of the power of the pharaohs in another sense—the power to organize and control a vast economic machine. The cost of building and maintaining them would have used all the state's resources and labor. And so the pyramids can be seen as a token of how rich and prosperous Egypt was under the Old Kingdom pharaohs, able to produce food to feed all its people and wealth to pay for its great temples and monuments.

It is extraordinary to think that the pyramids were built using only primitive tools of copper and wood. Teams of sweating, shouting workers would have dragged the great blocks on wooden sleds

DIVINE KHAFRA
This life-size statue of Khafra, builder of the Second Pyramid, with the wings of Horus protecting him, is a masterpiece of Old Kingdom art. Using a hard stone called diorite, the sculptor has superbly captured an air of god-like serenity on the pharaoh's face.

BIG HEAVE

Sleds were the quickest way to move heavy blocks, and the pace of work was fast. To build the Great Pyramid in 20 years, about 340 blocks were laid each day. An experiment at Giza in the 1990s proved that this was not impossible. It found that teams of fewer than 20 men could quickly drag a 2.5-ton block.

from quarries in the desert, hauling on long ropes. They may have used milk, or perhaps Nile mud, to make the runners slippery.

At the pyramid, the men heaved each stone up the sides and into place. How they did this is one of the great mysteries of ancient Egypt. It is probable that some type of great ramp made from sand and crushed stone was used, but no one is sure. However it was done, it must have been a back-breaking job, since each stone block weighed more than 40 adults.

THE PYRAMID RISES

No one is sure how blocks were hauled to the top of the pyramid. Most likely a ramp was used that clung to the face, like this one. The pyramid may have been built in steps in order to support a ramp.

It would have taken some 20 years to build each pyramid. The regular workforce of skilled laborers probably numbered only about 4,000. But thousands of farm workers came to help on the site when the annual Nile flood prevented them from working on their fields. We know that they formed gangs because there are graffiti on the stones of some pyramids that say "the Green Gang" or "the Western Gang." There may have been friendly competition between them, or they may have formed fraternities in the townships to which they returned each evening. They seem to have been fed well on a diet of meat, bread, and fish. Beside one pyramid, archaeologists have found the remains of a bakery and a fish-processing factory. As well as the work gangs, the pyramid towns also housed potters and brick-makers, masons and diggers. The pyramids would have provided work, too, for craftsmen such as scribes and painters. Merchants would have supplied food.

But there were other Egyptian monuments besides the pyramids. The son of Khufu, builder of the Great Pyramid, was named Khafra. He built the Second Pyramid at Giza, which stands close to Khufu's monument, but he is perhaps best known as the creator of the Great Sphinx. The largest statue ever carved by an ancient civilization, the Sphinx is a little under 200 ft (60 m) in length and more than 65 ft (20 m) high. It has the body of a great lion and the face of a pharaoh wearing a royal headdress.

CASING AND FINISHING
Working from the top down, teams of masons finished off the pyramid by fitting smooth limestone casing blocks. To measure the angle of the pyramid slope, the masons used a plumb line or a square.

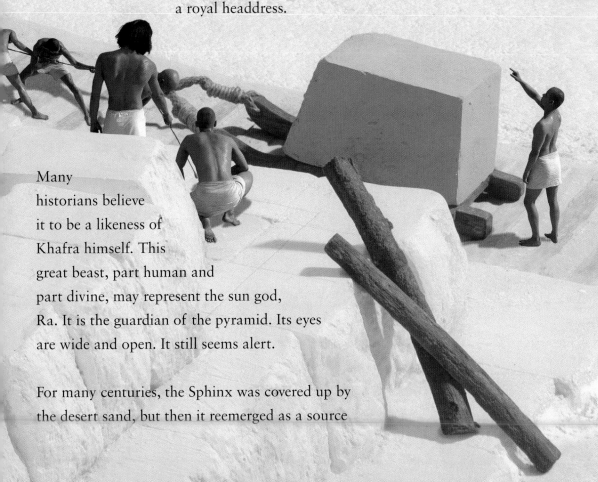

Many historians believe it to be a likeness of Khafra himself. This great beast, part human and part divine, may represent the sun god, Ra. It is the guardian of the pyramid. Its eyes are wide and open. It still seems alert.

For many centuries, the Sphinx was covered up by the desert sand, but then it reemerged as a source of wonder. Its beard and nose are now gone, and it has suffered from the continual wear of wind and sand, but it is still one of the most extraordinary sights in the world. It is a token of the beliefs of humankind from 4,500 years ago, and still has the capacity to inspire awe.

The Sphinx is part of great a complex of buildings built by Khafra that includes a valley temple linked by a causeway to a mortuary temple. The Sphinx temple functioned like a vast cosmic clock, with 24 statues and 24 pillars to mark the hours of the day and night. At the spring and fall equinoxes, when day and night are of equal length, the rays of the rising sun penetrate the innermost sanctum—or holy place—of the temple and bring it to life, lighting it with its beams. It is another memorial to the sun god, Ra, whose great stone statue lies outside.

PYRAMID GUARDIAN
Carved from a huge outcrop of limestone, the Sphinx is the largest sculpture to survive from the ancient world. The pyramid workers may have seen the shape of a sphinx in leftover rock at their quarry, and carved it as a tribute to their pharaoh, Khafra.

The son of Khafra, Menkaura, built the Third Pyramid at Giza, but it is less than half the size of the Great Pyramid. According to the accounts of Greek historians, writing 2,000 years later, Menkaura was a more merciful ruler than Khufu or Khafra, whose great building works are accompanied by stories of their cruelty and ruthlessness. Certainly, the superb surviving statues of Menkaura depict him with an intelligent and kindly face.

The later pharaohs of the Fourth Dynasty, and those of the Fifth and Sixth Dynasties, continued the tradition of pyramid-building, but their pyramids were smaller still and not as well built. It is tempting to think that powerful pharaohs built large pyramids, and less impressive rulers built smaller pyramids. But that is probably a false idea. Later pharaohs may simply not have reigned long enough to complete huge pyramids. There may have been another reason, too. Pyramids were becoming less important. A new type of building was taking priority in Egypt—the temple of the sun.

ROYAL COUPLE
This remarkable statue shows Menkaura with his favorite wife. The queen is hugging her husband lovingly. Human touches like this are rare in Egyptian art, which is usually very formal.

CHAPTER THREE

Decline of the *old* kingdom

The pharaohs of the Fifth Dynasty (2494–2345 BCE) are known as the Sun Kings. During their period of rule they took the cult of the sun god, Ra, to new heights. The Sixth Dynasty that followed was the last dynasty of the Old Kingdom.

USERKAF, THE FIRST PHARAOH of the Fifth Dynasty, built the first of the temples of the sun that marked this religious change. It had a great enclosure surrounded by a limestone wall. In the middle was a structure called an obelisk—a pillar of stone with a pyramid-shaped top. The obelisk stood on a stone base or podium and soared upward toward the sun. In front of it was an altar, on which animals were sacrificed. Close by was the barque, or boat, of the sun god, which magically allowed the sun to sail across the skies each day. Paintings decorated the inside walls of the sun temples. Among them were pictures of animals and birds. The Egyptians loved to depict the details of the natural world, and these scenes, particularly the birds, are painted with lifelike accuracy. In a country dominated by

◄ Fifth Dynasty tomb painting of the sun god, Ra-Harakhty

the brightness of sun and sand, bathed in an endless white light, the play of brilliant color and subtle shape was especially delightful.

There were many kings in the Fifth Dynasty, some of whom reigned for only a short time. The reign of Unas, the last of the dynasty, seems to have been marked by famine in Egypt. These unhappy times extended into the Sixth Dynasty (2345–2181 BCE), and there are signs that the royal household was troubled. Teti, the first of the dynasty, was murdered by his bodyguard, and one of the wives of his son and successor, Pepi I, plotted the death of her husband (the pharaohs had several wives but one principal queen known as Great Royal Wife). Pepi I discovered the plot, and his wife was arrested and tried. She may have been forced to commit suicide by taking poison, one of the standard methods of punishment in ancient Egypt.

Pepi I went on to reign for 50 years. He has the good fortune to be portrayed in the first life-size copper statue to have survived the ages.

ANIMAL SCENES
Sun temples were adorned with vivid scenes like this one, showing the diversity of wildlife among the papyrus marshes.

PEPI I
Though heavily corroded, the king's face is still sharp and lifelike on this 4,300-year-old copper statue. His crown, long lost, would have been made separately from gilded plaster.

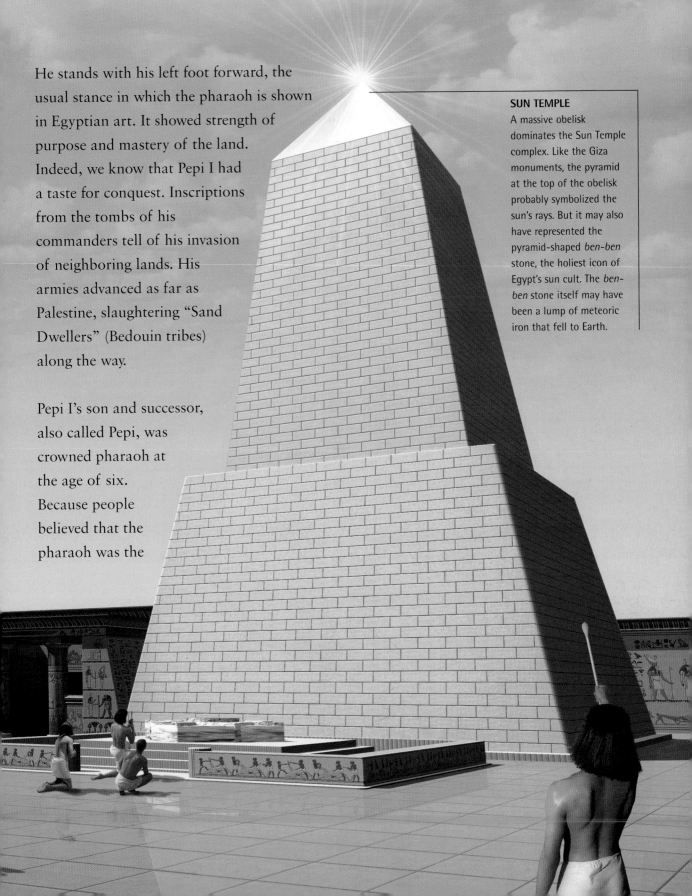

He stands with his left foot forward, the usual stance in which the pharaoh is shown in Egyptian art. It showed strength of purpose and mastery of the land. Indeed, we know that Pepi I had a taste for conquest. Inscriptions from the tombs of his commanders tell of his invasion of neighboring lands. His armies advanced as far as Palestine, slaughtering "Sand Dwellers" (Bedouin tribes) along the way.

Pepi I's son and successor, also called Pepi, was crowned pharaoh at the age of six. Because people believed that the pharaoh was the

SUN TEMPLE
A massive obelisk dominates the Sun Temple complex. Like the Giza monuments, the pyramid at the top of the obelisk probably symbolized the sun's rays. But it may also have represented the pyramid-shaped *ben-ben* stone, the holiest icon of Egypt's sun cult. The *ben-ben* stone itself may have been a lump of meteoric iron that fell to Earth.

INFANT PHARAOH
This small alabaster statuette shows the infant Pepi II sitting on his mother's lap. Pepi is shown as a miniature pharaoh, wearing his royal *nemes* headdress.

son of Horus, and a god living on the earth, it did not matter at what age he ascended to the throne. That is why some pharaohs reigned for a very long time. Pepi II himself reigned for longer than any other king in the history of the world—an astonishing 94 years, according to modern calculations. It is perhaps because he lived for so long that Egypt began to show signs of weariness and weakness at this time.

During Pepi II's long reign, the administration grew slack and inefficient, and the upkeep of Egypt's foreign provinces drained the state's wealth. But worst of all, it seems that authority had begun to slip from the hands of the pharaoh. The kings of the Fifth and Sixth Dynasties had given away some of their powers to local nobles and provincial governors, and had left the day-to-day running of the country to the growing

numbers of administrators. Egypt had always relied upon administrators (people we would call civil servants or bureaucrats) and now had more of them than ever before. The royal household itself contained a vizier and a treasurer, each of whom had armies of scribes and officials reporting to them, in addition to the butlers, stewards, cooks, servants, guards, heralds, nurses, and priests who worked in the palaces. The pharaoh alone would have directly employed many thousands of people.

From the earliest times, the government had involved itself in every aspect of life to ensure that Egypt remained prosperous and stable. The smallest details of people's lives were supervised. There were civil servants to organize the storage and distribution of grain from public granaries (grain stores), civil servants to look after the royal treasuries of gold and precious stones, and civil servants in charge of the army's supply of weapons. There were departments for foreign trade, for the building of tombs, temples, and pyramids, and for taxation. Officials made sure the dams and

FISH QUOTA
A fisherman had to catch 5,000 fish a year or be punished for his failure. Every trade in Egypt was controlled by the state.

KEEPERS OF RECORDS
Scribes were privileged because they were among the few who could read and write. They recorded many aspects of life.

NILOMETERS
Ancient nilometers like this one, used to record the river's flood level, continued to be useful up until 1971, when the building of the massive Aswan Dam put a stop to the Nile's annual flood.

canals that controlled the Nile were kept in a state of good repair and cared for the "nilometers," a series of marks carved on the sides of stone walls to measure the height of the annual flood. Since taxes were calculated according to the level the water reached each year, this was a matter of great importance. If the Nile reached its "ideal" level, the farmers would have a good harvest and could pay more tax.

Egypt was divided into administrative districts, or provinces, known as "nomes." Each nome had mayors, priests, overseers (supervisors), and a governor of its own. The governor was often the high priest of the local temple, too, so that politics and religion were deeply mingled. Legal matters were settled in the local courts of justice.

All land belonged—in theory—to the pharaoh. The concept of money was unknown, and so civil servants were paid with estates or plots of land on which they grew all the produce they needed for life and trade. They were trained as scribes, too, because all servants of the state had to be able to read, write, and calculate figures. Official posts usually remained within families, with sons following their fathers into government. Civil servants did not pay taxes and enjoyed many other privileges. The rest of the population also worked at jobs

CIVIL SERVANTS
In this harvesting scene, scribes can be seen busily recording the quantity of grain. They did this in order to work out how much tax the farmer had to pay the state. Payment would be made in grain.

that were handed down from father to son. Some were potters or masons, others carpenters or goldsmiths working in the great temple workshops, but most people toiled in the fields or herded animals.

The death of Pepi II in 2184 BCE marked the end of the Old Kingdom and the line of pharaohs who ruled from Memphis. The old man had probably outlived all his heirs. As a result, his death sparked a crisis in which the country's fragile unity fell apart. We know almost nothing of the pharaohs of the Seventh and Eighth Dynasties, because it seems that central order had collapsed, with terrible consequences for the whole of Egypt. There is also evidence of a great famine at this

POWERFUL PRIEST
This remarkably lifelike statue, carved from sycamore wood, represents a chief priest named Ka-Aper. Officials like Ka-Aper governed the administrative districts and temples of the Old Kingdom, and held enormous political power.

FAMINE
This Old Kingdom relief shows people dying of hunger after the Nile failed to flood. The Nile's failure may have been caused by a cooling climate.

time. Accounts speak of the fear of hunger looming over the people of Egypt. Some historians believe that the Nile failed to flood for several years, causing severe food shortages. There were episodes of disease; wars broke out between provincial governors, and thieves broke into tombs to steal the treasures buried with the dead—one of the worst crimes imaginable in ancient Egypt. Egyptologists suspect that the Great Pyramid itself may have been broken into during this period.

For 1,000 years, Egypt had been peaceful, prosperous, and stable. Its civilization had flourished in every sphere of life, reaching a pinnacle of technological achievement during the Pyramid Age. The breakdown of order and the chaos that followed came as a terrible shock to the Egyptians. Such a thing had never happened before. But as we will see, violent swings between periods of order and periods of anarchy were to become a feature of life in the Nile Valley over the next 2,000 years.

Although the Old Kingdom was over, its achievements were never forgotten by the people of Egypt. Later generations looked back at the Old Kingdom as a golden age. The Egyptians always regarded their past as holy. Just as their elaborate tombs celebrated a cult of the dead, so they worshiped the past life of their country.

But the Egyptians not only celebrated their past, but copied it. Two thousand years after

the collapse of the Old Kingdom, the rulers of Egypt continued to revive its ancient customs. In later centuries, sculptors, artists, and tomb-builders were still using the styles of the Old Kingdom. Even the clothing fashions and writing of the past were imitated. It was a way of drawing upon the energy and the inspiration of the past to uphold the present. To the ancient Egyptian mind, the life of the past could always be reborn.

MODEL STYLE .
This painted limestone relief shows a princess seated at a table piled with bread. The image is typical of the superb quality of Old Kingdom illustration style, which continued to serve as the standard for artists throughout ancient Egypt's history.

The unhappy time that followed the Old Kingdom is called the "First Intermediate Period" (2181–2055 BCE). This is because it falls between the end of the Old Kingdom and the beginning of a period known as the Middle Kingdom. It was a time when chaos reigned. Egypt was no longer a unified country. The pharaohs of the short-lived Seventh and Eighth Dynasties were followed by the equally

Egyptian time

The Egyptians thought of time as a curling snake, with the indication that it could circle back upon itself. Time flowed not from past to future, but in circles or cycles. Even at the time of the Old Kingdom, Egypt was already very ancient. Records of events went far back into the time of legend and myth, so it is possible that the Egyptians recognized patterns or cycles in their history. Numerous lists were made to record reigns and events. Historians today still use a record composed in 300 BCE by an Egyptian priest named Manetho. He divided Egypt's long history into the dynasties of the pharaohs.

King's name appears in cartouche

Snake symbolized endless time

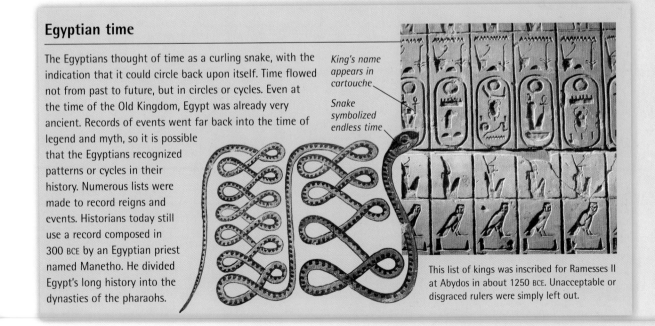

This list of kings was inscribed for Ramesses II at Abydos in about 1250 BCE. Unacceptable or disgraced rulers were simply left out.

shadowy figures of the Ninth and Tenth Dynasties, who betwe
them ruled for about 135 years. Historians have very little evide
their reigns. We know that they moved their capital from Mem
the northern city of Heracleopolis, but their power did not stre
over all of Egypt.

During these uncertain times, the provinces and cities of Egypt
more independent. Provincial governors and nobles gained in p
and importance and built much larger and more richly decorat
tombs for themselves. One such tomb belonged to a noble nam
Ankhtifi. He was the governor of two nomes in the south of E
so he was very powerful indeed. An inscription on his tomb de
his heroic efforts to clothe the naked and feed the
hungry during a time of famine.

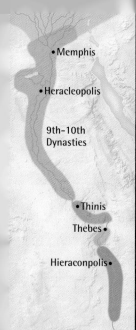

• Memphis

• Heracleopolis

9th-10th
Dynasties

• Thinis

Thebes •

Hieraconpolis •

HE LAND DIVIDED
his map shows how
ragmented Egypt
ecame during the
First Intermediate Period.
Political control was
divided between the
Ninth and Tenth Dynasty
rulers in Lower Egypt
(pink area), and the
governors of Thinis,
Thebes, and Hieraconpolis
n Upper Egypt.

HOME FOR THE DEAD
Behind the pillars of a
saff tomb is an angled
roof known as a portico.
The tomb's design
imitated the wooden
verandas and ceiling
beams of Egyptian homes.

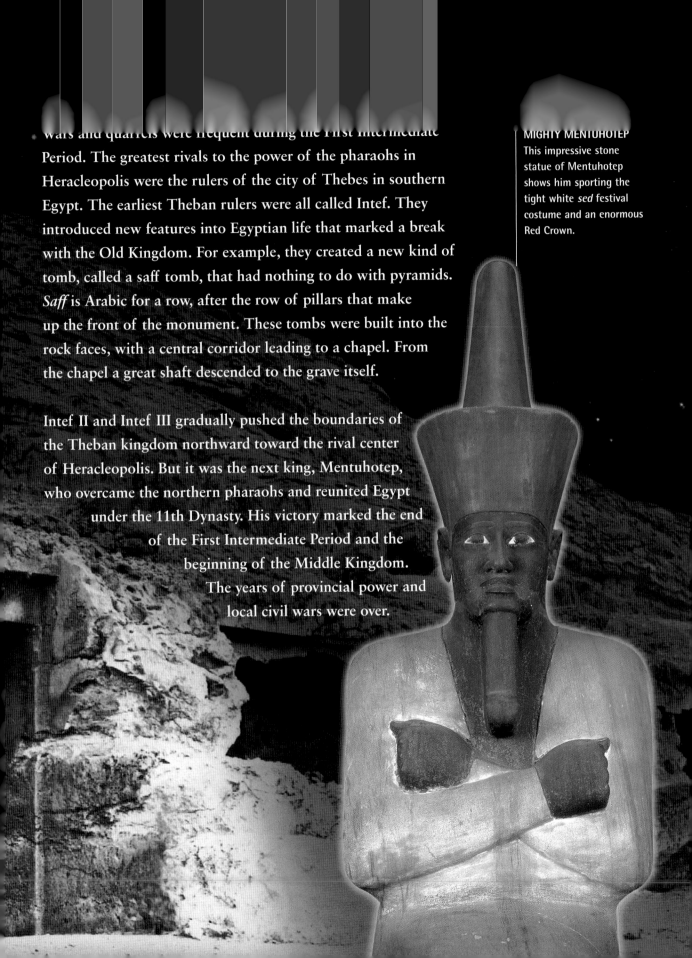

Wars and quarrels were frequent during the First Intermediate Period. The greatest rivals to the power of the pharaohs in Heracleopolis were the rulers of the city of Thebes in southern Egypt. The earliest Theban rulers were all called Intef. They introduced new features into Egyptian life that marked a break with the Old Kingdom. For example, they created a new kind of tomb, called a saff tomb, that had nothing to do with pyramids. *Saff* is Arabic for a row, after the row of pillars that make up the front of the monument. These tombs were built into the rock faces, with a central corridor leading to a chapel. From the chapel a great shaft descended to the grave itself.

Intef II and Intef III gradually pushed the boundaries of the Theban kingdom northward toward the rival center of Heracleopolis. But it was the next king, Mentuhotep, who overcame the northern pharaohs and reunited Egypt under the 11th Dynasty. His victory marked the end of the First Intermediate Period and the beginning of the Middle Kingdom. The years of provincial power and local civil wars were over.

MIGHTY MENTUHOTEP
This impressive stone statue of Mentuhotep shows him sporting the tight white *sed* festival costume and an enormous Red Crown.

CHAPTER FOUR

The *middle* kingdom

Mentuhotep reigned for 51 years. Such was his success that 1,000 years after his death, Egyptians still worshiped and honored him as the founder of the Middle Kingdom, a period of stability that lasted more than 250 years.

H E WAS SELF-CONFIDENT ENOUGH to declare himself a god during his own lifetime and named one of his temples the House of Millions of Years. Mentuhotep restored the cult of the pharaoh, in other words. There are many surviving images of him in paint and in stone. In one temple he is shown taking part in the *sed* festival, when the pharaoh ran a course around a courtyard in front of his assembled people. The ceremony was a way of miraculously renewing the divine strength of the pharaoh and took place in the 30th year of his reign. In another temple, Mentuhotep is seated on his throne in majesty, holding the ritual flail in his right hand.

It was only to be expected that Mentuhotep would plan a magnificent final resting place for himself. The

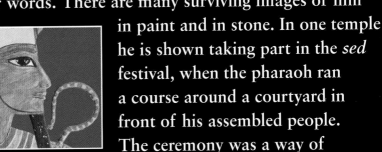

◀ Black granite statue of Amenemhat III as a sphinx

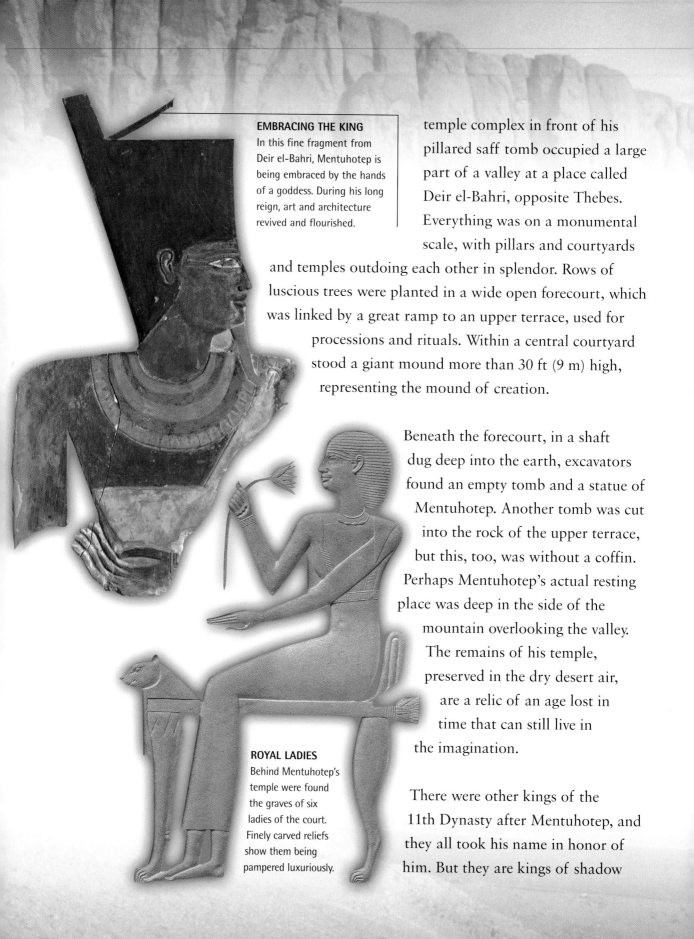

temple complex in front of his pillared saff tomb occupied a large part of a valley at a place called Deir el-Bahri, opposite Thebes. Everything was on a monumental scale, with pillars and courtyards and temples outdoing each other in splendor. Rows of luscious trees were planted in a wide open forecourt, which was linked by a great ramp to an upper terrace, used for processions and rituals. Within a central courtyard stood a giant mound more than 30 ft (9 m) high, representing the mound of creation.

Beneath the forecourt, in a shaft dug deep into the earth, excavators found an empty tomb and a statue of Mentuhotep. Another tomb was cut into the rock of the upper terrace, but this, too, was without a coffin. Perhaps Mentuhotep's actual resting place was deep in the side of the mountain overlooking the valley. The remains of his temple, preserved in the dry desert air, are a relic of an age lost in time that can still live in the imagination.

There were other kings of the 11th Dynasty after Mentuhotep, and they all took his name in honor of him. But they are kings of shadow

ROYAL LADIES
Behind Mentuhotep's temple were found the graves of six ladies of the court. Finely carved reliefs show them being pampered luxuriously.

and darkness. The records tell us little about them, except that they maintained the defenses of the country and traded with their neighbors. The 11th Dynasty came to an end when a man named Amenemhat, who was probably the vizier or first minister for the last of the Mentuhoteps, became king himself. Amenemhat was from a relatively humble background, but had worked his way up through the ranks of the royal household to attain the golden Horus throne

of Egypt. So although the pharaoh was considered to be a god living on the earth, the route to power was open to someone born outside the royal family. We do not know whether Amenemhat succeeded because the previous pharaoh died without an heir, or whether he seized the crown by force. Whatever the truth, he proved himself a highly capable ruler.

TEMPLE TREES
This relief depicts the types of trees, such as sycamores and tamarisks, that were planted in rows before Mentuhotep's temple.

The 12th Dynasty founded by Amenemhat lasted for about 200 years (1985–1795 BCE), although we are not sure of the precise dates. The pharaohs of this dynasty began the custom of ruling alongside a co-regent, who was their chosen successor. This was a way of ensuring an easy handover of power on the death of the pharaoh. But the practice has made it difficult for historians of ancient Egypt to work out the length of each pharaoh's reign.

EXOTIC NUBIA
Nubia was a source for many types of exotic goods. This painting shows Nubians carrying gold rings, chunks of red jasper, giraffe tails, leopard skins, and ebony logs.

LUXURY GOODS
This gold-handled sword has a Middle Eastern design, and may have been imported as a luxury. The mirror has a surface of polished bronze.

The new pharaoh traded with his neighbors and made Egypt stable and prosperous. The Nile and its surroundings provided almost everything that the people of Egypt needed, but in exchange for grain and gold, the pharaohs acquired luxury goods from abroad. Weapons, furniture, and lapis lazuli (a highly prized blue stone) were imported from Mesopotamia; cedar wood was brought from Lebanon (good timber was always in short supply in Egypt). Supplies of incense, used in religious ceremonies, came from the mysterious kingdom of Punt to the southeast of Egypt, while from Nubia there flowed a stream of exotic goods such as panther skins, ostrich feathers, elephant tusks, and giraffe tails for use as fly whisks.

Amenemhat himself reigned for almost 30 years. To mark the beginning of a new reign and a new dynasty, Amenemhat gave himself a name meaning "rebirth." He also moved the capital

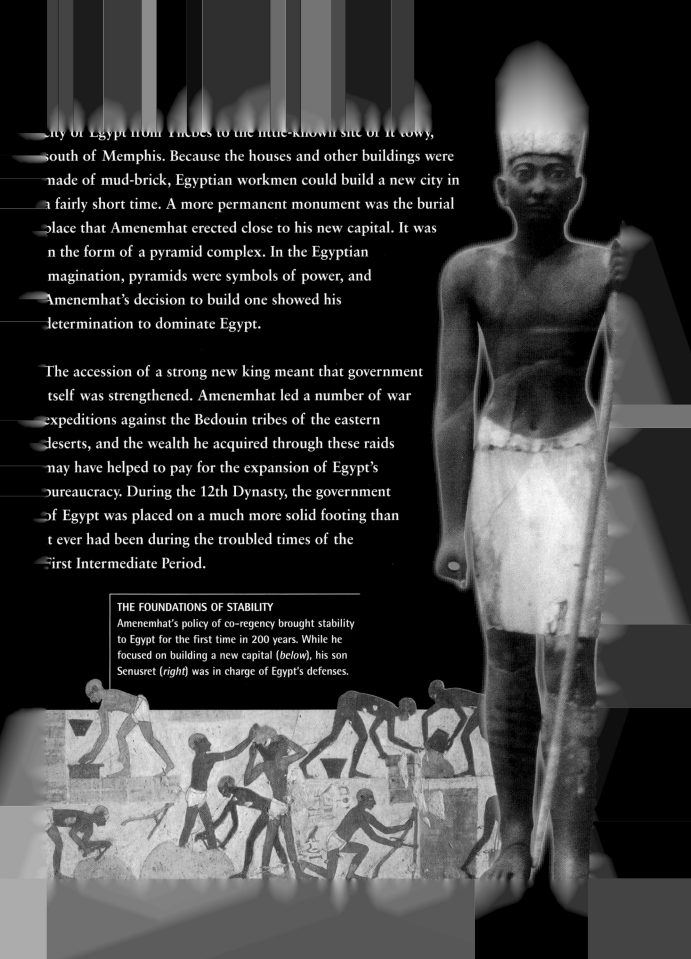

city of Egypt from Thebes to the little-known site of It-towy, south of Memphis. Because the houses and other buildings were made of mud-brick, Egyptian workmen could build a new city in a fairly short time. A more permanent monument was the burial place that Amenemhat erected close to his new capital. It was in the form of a pyramid complex. In the Egyptian imagination, pyramids were symbols of power, and Amenemhat's decision to build one showed his determination to dominate Egypt.

The accession of a strong new king meant that government itself was strengthened. Amenemhat led a number of war expeditions against the Bedouin tribes of the eastern deserts, and the wealth he acquired through these raids may have helped to pay for the expansion of Egypt's bureaucracy. During the 12th Dynasty, the government of Egypt was placed on a much more solid footing than it ever had been during the troubled times of the First Intermediate Period.

THE FOUNDATIONS OF STABILITY
Amenemhat's policy of co-regency brought stability to Egypt for the first time in 200 years. While he focused on building a new capital (*below*), his son Senusret (*right*) was in charge of Egypt's defenses.

RUBBLE REMAINS

A pile of sand and rubble is all that remains of Amenemhat I's pyramid at Lisht in Lower Egypt. The core was built of small stone blocks, many taken from Old Kingdom monuments at Giza. The smooth outer casing of white Tura limestone has long since been stolen.

Amenemhat's interest in the practicalities of day-to-day rule suggests that he and his successors were more concerned with life in this world than in life after death. Perhaps this reflected a historical change in the long course of Egyptian beliefs. Throughout the 12th Dynasty, the pharaohs put a much greater effort into helping people's daily lives by building dams and boosting agriculture than into planning elaborate memorials for the grave. They continued to build pyramids for themselves, but these were on a much smaller scale than those of the Old Kingdom.

It is perhaps unfortunate, then, that Amenemhat was murdered. A text, supposedly from the lips of the murdered pharaoh himself, recounts the killing. "I was asleep upon my bed... As I awoke I encountered fighting, and I discovered that it was an assault by my bodyguard." No doubt he was killed as a result of a palace plot. There may have been some who muttered that it was a fitting end for someone who had no right to the throne in the first place.

Amenemhat's son, Senusret, was away on a military expedition in the west when he heard the news of his father's death. So he hurried back

ARMY ON THE MARCH

These wooden models, found in the tomb of a Middle Kingdom general, give us an accurate idea of how soldiers of the time must have looked. They marched in formations of 40 or 50 men, armed with spears and hide shields.

to Egypt, and immediately put down any sign of internal mutiny. As Senusret I, he reigned for 45 years. Like his father, Senusret was often at war. He conquered Lower Nubia, the region to the south of Egypt, and turned it into an Egyptian province. He sent trading expeditions to Syria and other distant lands. As a mark of his power and importance, Senusret I set up many monuments and temples throughout the lands under his rule. In so doing, he helped to widen the influence of Osiris, his favorite god.

All Egyptians knew the story of Osiris, just as Christians know the story of the birth of Jesus and Muslims know the story of Muhammad. According to myth, the god Osiris had once ruled Egypt as a wise and just king, but was killed by his jealous brother, Seth. Seth ripped apart the body of Osiris and scattered his limbs over all Egypt. But the goddess Isis, the wife and sister of Osiris, miraculously restored the torn body and made Osiris whole once more. Isis and Osiris then raised a son, Horus, who triumphed over Seth and banished him to the desert wastes, where he became the god of chaos and evil.

ROYAL TRAINING
Senusret I had ruled for ten years as co-regent with his father before becoming king himself. As a result, he had been trained well and ruled wisely. He led many military expeditions beyond Egypt's borders, including to the remote Western Desert oases.

GOD OF THE DEAD
Osiris was usually shown wrapped in a white shroud. Mummies were prepared in the same way as the body of Osiris had been long ago. If all went well, the mummy would "become an Osiris" and live for ever.

As a result of his revival and restoration, Osiris became the god of rebirth and the protector of the Nile, whose annual renewal watered Egypt. But Osiris also became the god of the underworld, where rebirth was part of the pattern of destiny. His kingdom, known as the "Field of Reeds," lay beyond the perilous regions below the earth. Those souls fortunate enough to enter would inhabit a place of eternal spring, where the flowers and fruits of the field flourished exceedingly. In the Field of Reeds, every poor person would have a plot of land, while the pharaoh sailed across the heavens in the barque of Ra.

Central to the cult of Osiris promoted by Senusret was the belief that both rich and

THE DEATH OF OSIRIS
This image depicts a famous scene from the legend of Osiris. The jealous Seth had secretly made a beautiful casket to the measurements of Osiris's body. At a feast, Seth offered the casket to whichever guest fitted inside. When Osiris lay down in it, Seth nailed the casket shut and threw it into the Nile, which carried it out to sea.

Dead person appears before the god Anubis

Jury of gods sits in judgment

Anubis weighs the heart against the Feather of Truth

Thoth takes notes and delivers verdict

The monster Ammut lies in wait

Weighing the heart

To enter the kingdom of Osiris, a dead person had to answer questions about his or her life in front of a jury of gods. The person's heart was then weighed against the Feather of Truth on a pair of scales. If the scales balanced, it meant that the person had lived virtuously and could enter the afterlife. A terrible fate awaited those bad people whose scales did not balance. Their hearts were thrown to the monster Ammut, known as "the Devourer of the Dead," and their souls were extinguished forever.

poor alike could share in the delights of eternity. All Egyptians could be saved or restored to good fortune after death—the afterlife no longer belonged to the pharaoh alone. Mystery plays performed at festivals dedicated to Osiris celebrated the god's glorious destiny. His image was displayed throughout the kingdom as a "mummiform" king—that is, as a pharaoh in the shape of a mummy. He wore a long white cloak and the White Crown of Upper Egypt, together with the crook and the flail as the symbols of kingship and fertility. His face was colored black or green, the sacred colors of fertility and rebirth.

The reign of Senusret I was a time when literature flourished in Egypt. Some writings of this period can be described as "wisdom literature." In *The Instructions of Amenemhat*, the murdered king sets out to teach his successor about the perils of being a pharaoh. He advises him to rule his subjects strongly and watch that

FIELD OF REEDS
In this well-known tomb painting, a New Kingdom noble and his wife are happily at work gathering in the harvest. This is just how Egyptians imagined life in the Field of Reeds— except that the wheat grew much taller!

those closest to him do not betray him. *The Story of Sinuhe* recounts the fable of a young man who flees Egypt, in fear of his life for a supposed act of treason, but returns in old age to be honored by his country. The moral of this tale is that Egypt is his real mother, with whom he is reunited in the tomb.

The most important collection of writing surviving to us from Egyptian times is the Book of the Dead, the handbook for the traveler journeying through the underworld. A copy of the Book of the Dead, written on a piece of papyrus, was sometimes rolled up and placed with the body in the coffin. Egyptians believed that it had originally been written by Thoth, the god of writing and wisdom. It contained about 200 magic spells to be used by the departed in order to navigate the dangers of the afterlife. There were spells for summoning the boat of the gods, for changing shape, and for answering the judges who were to give their verdict on your life. There were spells to open the gates of death's

STRICT TEACHING
Privileged Egyptian children went to school between the ages of four and twelve. Most lessons were probably very tedious. Pupils were not taught to think for themselves. Lack of respect or questioning the teacher's reasoning were punished with a beating.

kingdom, guarded by demons—the departed had to advance toward the demon and say, "I know you and I know your name."

Other writings are collections of proverbs or sayings that tell people how to behave in a society where everyone was supposed to know his or her place. "Be polite to strangers and to guests." "Do not brag or be over-confident." "Be content with who you are and what you have achieved and do not desire your neighbor's wealth." "Nourish your own gifts." Schoolboys were expected to learn these proverbs as part of their lessons. They scrawled the sayings down on scraps of papyrus and broken pieces of slate or pottery in order to memorize them. Archaeologists have found many of these discarded scraps, and so the proverbs have come down to us.

Schools were maintained by the temples and were restricted to boys from privileged families, who were taught reading, writing, and mathematics in order to become priests or scribes or administrators—in other words, the leading members of Egyptian society. But most children did not go to school. Boys were taught to be farmers, brick-makers, carpenters, or masons by their fathers, and girls were trained by their mothers to run the home.

Perhaps the most remarkable pharaoh of the Middle Kingdom was the mighty Senusret III, who reigned from 1874 to 1855 BCE. He was said to have been almost 6 ft 6 in (2 m) tall, so his great size must have added to his kingly power. Senusret III strengthened royal government and reduced the

HIEROGLYPH PRACTICE
Hieroglyphs were not easy to draw, and needed a lot of practice. Here, a pupil has gotten carried away drawing a duckling hieroglyph. He has also drawn a lion's head, which is used in a scene in the Book of the Dead.

HIDDEN BOOK
This wooden statue of Osiris was placed in a tomb. It has a secret compartment where a rolled-up copy of the Book of the Dead was hidden.

NUBIAN STRONGHOLD
Senusret III's Nubian forts had bastions, moats, and rounded towers built with arrow slits, very similar to those of medieval Europe.

independence of the nobles. He fought campaigns against Nubia, and built a chain of forts along the southern frontier. One of Senusret's great achievements was to build a canal around an outcrop of rocks and waterfalls—known as a cataract—so that boats could travel freely up and down the Nile. He had various inscriptions carved to celebrate his greatness, including one that commemorates his battles against the Nubians: "I took away their people, advanced upon their wells, killed their bulls."

The statues of this pharaoh are some of the best known in all Egyptian art. He is typically depicted with large ears, brooding, watchful eyes, and a down-turned mouth. His look of severity stresses his great labors on behalf of his people. Images of the pharaohs now showed them not as godlike figures but as human beings of great power. This did not stop the pharaohs from becoming objects of cult worship, however. Senusret III was still worshiped in Nubia hundreds of years after his death.

His son, Amenemhat III, seems to have reigned in peace as a result of the conquests of his father. He built two pyramids in memory of his life upon the earth. The one containing his body, at a place called Hawara, was designed with many secret passages and trap doors, corridors and sliding panels, false doors and dead-end tunnels. This maze of limestone and mud-brick, known as "the Labyrinth," was intended to confuse tomb-robbers in their search for gold and treasures. But it did not deter them. At some time in the distant past, the tomb was

STERN PHARAOH
Senusret III looks thoughtful and stern in this statue. The large ears were a feature of sculpture from this period.

THE "BLACK PYRAMID"

Amenemhat III is pictured here against the ruins of his first pyramid, at Dahshur. The monument's limestone casing was plundered long ago, leaving the mud-brick core to erode into an eerie, mountainlike structure.

robbed, the bodies taken, and the coffins burned. The one thing greater than human power is human ingenuity. The lowliest thief can eventually outwit the most feared pharaoh.

The last pharaoh of the 12th Dynasty was a woman, Queen Sobeknefru (1799–1795 BCE). She may have ruled as a co-regent to Amenemhat IV before assuming supreme power. One of her titles was "the Female Hawk, beloved of Ra," and on statues she is shown wearing both male and female costume, emphasizing her status as a female leader. Women pharaohs were rare but not unique in Egyptian history. And as we will see, Sobeknefru was neither the last, nor the most powerful, of Egypt's formidable female pharaohs.

LABYRINTH LAYOUT

This image shows how the plan of Amenemhat III's second pyramid, at Hawara, may have looked. The vast labyrinth lies before it.

CHAPTER FIVE

Chaos *and* reunification

The death of Queen Sobeknefru sparked another period of confusion in the chronicles of Egyptian history. The next dynasty, the 13th, had about 70 minor kings; the rulers of the 14th Dynasty are even more obscure. Power was breaking down.

IT WAS THE BEGINNING of the Second Intermediate Period (1650–1550 BCE), when a divided Egypt was ruled by many kings. Out of this chaos emerged the one result that many Egyptians had most feared. A group of foreigners known as the Hyksos came to dominate much of Egypt and to establish their own line of kings. It would once have been unthinkable—pharaohs who were not Egyptian—but it had come to pass. Their dynasty, which is the 15th Dynasty, lasted for 100 years. Historians are not sure where the Hyksos originally came from. The name "Hyksos" itself is an Egyptian word meaning "rulers from foreign lands." They were probably immigrants from Palestine, Syria, or Lebanon who had lived in Egypt for many generations and, by gradually acquiring wealth and influence, were able to rise to supreme power.

◄ Avenue of sphinxes at the temple of Karnak

SMALL BUT DEADLY
The first arrowheads were made of flint or hardwood. Later, bronze was used. Horseshoe-shaped points were designed to wound, while triangular points were meant to kill.

The Hyksos pharaohs established their capital at Avaris, in the Delta region of Egypt where they had originally settled and where they were strongest. Although they were foreigners, they made a great effort to identify themselves with their Egyptian predecessors by adopting Egyptian royal names and by worshiping the sun god, Ra. But they also picked another Egyptian god as their own protecting deity. This was Seth, the god of storms, chaos, and deserts, chosen perhaps because these settlers had originally come from desert regions. Despite their efforts to present themselves as Egypt's rightful rulers, the Hyksos did have some very different customs from the

ARCHERS ON THE MARCH
The Hyksos introduced a new, longer type of bow designed to shoot arrows from moving chariots. Later pharaohs hired Nubian mercenaries, such as those shown in this model, as archers.

Egyptians. Perhaps the strangest was their practice of burying their favorite donkeys next to their tombs.

These foreign rulers introduced new elements into warfare, including the horse and chariot, which were previously unknown in Egypt. They were skilled archers, too, taking the art of the bow to new heights. No doubt they used their military expertise to bring large areas of the country under their control. The Hyksos understood that a successful pharaoh had also to be a good general.

The best known of the Hyksos pharaohs, Apepi, reigned for more than 40 years. His name is inscribed on many monuments, even those of earlier pharaohs, as if he were trying to draw some of their honor and glory upon himself. While Apepi's power spread across the north of the country, some minor Egyptian kings belonging to the 16th Dynasty ruled at the same time in the south, perhaps with the assent of the Hyksos. But the main rivals to the Hyksos were the rulers of Thebes, who eventually became the 17th Dynasty.

The Thebans refused to accept the Hyksos as pharaohs. One Theban king, Seqenenre, challenged their authority and organized two military expeditions against Avaris. He probably died during the second campaign. The mummy of his body bears terrible wounds on the face and head, which suggest that he may have been slain in battle. His mouth is open, showing his white teeth, and his hair is still black. It is a picture of violent death.

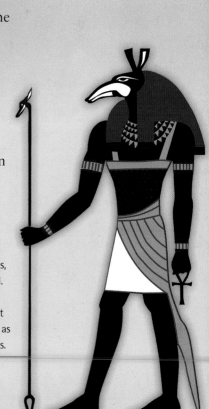

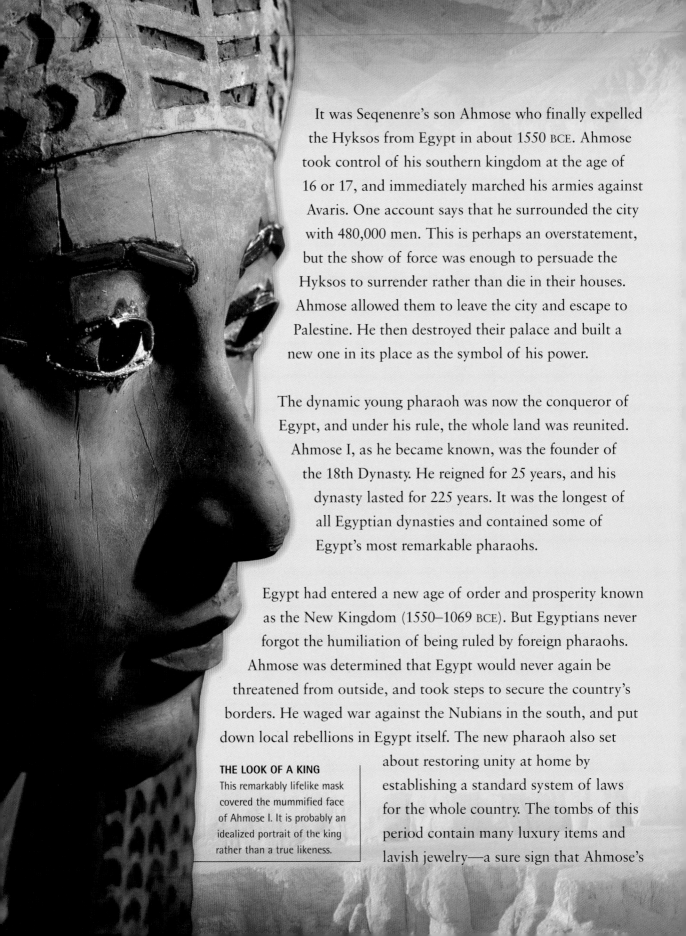

It was Seqenenre's son Ahmose who finally expelled the Hyksos from Egypt in about 1550 BCE. Ahmose took control of his southern kingdom at the age of 16 or 17, and immediately marched his armies against Avaris. One account says that he surrounded the city with 480,000 men. This is perhaps an overstatement, but the show of force was enough to persuade the Hyksos to surrender rather than die in their houses. Ahmose allowed them to leave the city and escape to Palestine. He then destroyed their palace and built a new one in its place as the symbol of his power.

The dynamic young pharaoh was now the conqueror of Egypt, and under his rule, the whole land was reunited. Ahmose I, as he became known, was the founder of the 18th Dynasty. He reigned for 25 years, and his dynasty lasted for 225 years. It was the longest of all Egyptian dynasties and contained some of Egypt's most remarkable pharaohs.

Egypt had entered a new age of order and prosperity known as the New Kingdom (1550–1069 BCE). But Egyptians never forgot the humiliation of being ruled by foreign pharaohs. Ahmose was determined that Egypt would never again be threatened from outside, and took steps to secure the country's borders. He waged war against the Nubians in the south, and put down local rebellions in Egypt itself. The new pharaoh also set about restoring unity at home by establishing a standard system of laws for the whole country. The tombs of this period contain many luxury items and lavish jewelry—a sure sign that Ahmose's

THE LOOK OF A KING
This remarkably lifelike mask covered the mummified face of Ahmose I. It is probably an idealized portrait of the king rather than a true likeness.

VALLEY OF THE KINGS
From about 1500 BCE, Egypt's kings were buried in a secret valley near Thebes, far from their old burial places in the north. Tombs like this one were cut deep into the cliffs of the valley, the entrance to which was guarded day and night.

policies were successful in creating wealth. Ahmose built temples and monuments at many sacred sites, including Memphis and Thebes, Karnak and Abydos. Many were devoted to Osiris and other gods, but the deity most favored by Ahmose was Amun, whose name means "the hidden one."

Amun was the local god of Thebes, but Ahmose now placed the whole country under the god's protection. Later pharaohs would claim to be the son of Amun, and consequently Thebes became the most sacred site in Egypt. Eventually, Amun was joined with the sun god, Ra, and became Amun-Ra, who was the lord of lords, the god of gods, the great one who existed before creation and who was creation.

No one knows where Ahmose's tomb lies. But his body has been found. The tombs of the New Kingdom pharaohs were dug deep into the rock at a place on the edge of the Western Desert called the Valley of the Kings. This sacred valley is overlooked by a mountain that in outline resembles a pyramid. It is the entrance to the underworld itself. Over the long period of the New Kingdom, almost 30 pharaohs were buried there. But by about 1000 BCE, a group of priests had become so concerned about tomb robberies in the valley that they gathered together a large number of mummies and reburied them in an empty tomb at nearby Deir el-Bahri. These bodies were found only at the end of the 19th century. There were 40 all together, including some of the most famous pharaohs of the New Kingdom. And with them was the mummy of Ahmose I.

GOD OF GODS
Amun-Ra was the most mysterious of the gods. He could not be seen or understood, even by the greatest scribes. He gave victory in battle and handed the sword of conquest to the great warrior pharaohs of the New Kingdom.

ETERNAL PEACE
The calm expression on Ahmose's face is still apparent after thousands of years. There are even hairs on his head.

THE FATHER OF MUMMIES
Anubis, the jackal-headed god of embalming, prepares
a mummy for the tomb. Jackals were linked to death
in the Egyptian imagination because they prowled
around cemeteries at night and scavenged for corpses.

A mummy is a preserved body. Mummies are so
associated with ancient Egypt that they have almost become its
symbol. Archaeologists have found the bodies of Egyptians dating
back more than 6,000 years. The bodies had dried out in the hot
desert sands and were thus naturally mummified. The Egyptians may
have discovered these mummies by accident and realized that drying
a body prevents it from rotting away. And so the idea came to them
of artificially preserving bodies. The first known artificial mummy
comes from the First Dynasty, approximately 5,000 years ago, when
the dead body was wrapped in linen bandages soaked in resin to
assist its preservation.

SERVANTS OF THE DEAD
In the tombs of the
better-off, the priests
placed little wooden
models of servants known
as shabtis ("answerers").
It was thought that when
the tomb was sealed, the
shabtis would magically
come alive to carry out
the orders of the dead.

Techniques of preserving, or embalming, bodies improved in the
Middle Kingdom, when it became common to remove the brain as
well as the other internal organs in order to slow down the process of
decay. But it was during the New Kingdom that the art of mummy-
making was perfected. The process was lengthy and complicated.
The embalmers dried out the body beneath a mound of special salt
called natron for up to

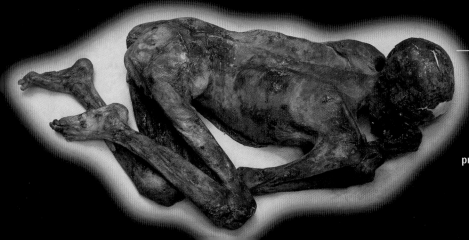

EGYPTIAN SAND MUMMY
Before mummification, Egyptians
buried their dead in sand pits.
The sand dried out the body and
prevented it from decaying. This
5,000-year-old man has well-
preserved skin, nails, and red hair.

40 days, and then rubbed it with resin and sweet-smelling oils. Only then did the long process of wrapping the corpse in linen bandages begin. Embalming was an honored trade, which passed down through generations of the same family.

The Egyptians mummified their dead because they believed that the *ka*, one of the spirits of the person, would return to the body after death. He or she could then consume the offerings of food left in the tomb. A special ritual performed before the funeral was known as "the Opening of the Mouth." This was a way of magically restoring the senses so that the corpse could be reborn into a new existence, able to eat, drink, and move around. All these ceremonies were part of the Egyptian cult of the dead, the belief that the dead still lived and flourished in the afterlife.

The tomb became the home of the corpse upon the earth, furnished with the familiar items of home life—everything from clothes and cosmetics to fans and wigs, as well as food and wine. In one tomb, archaeologists discovered pigeon stew and cooked fish, cheese and wild berries.

BROUGHT TO LIFE
Mourners wail and priests burn incense as the Opening of the Mouth ritual is performed upon a mummy, held upright by Anubis.

SOLAR SAIL
In this detail from an astronomical ceiling in the tomb of Ramesses VI, the sun god, Ra, sails the celestial sea in his barque. Around him are the gods of the underworld.

The cult of the dead explains why the royal tombs grew as large as they did, with all their labyrinthine passages and halls, chapels and chambers, shafts and corridors. These were palaces for eternity, where the dead king could continue his rituals in honor of the gods. In some royal tombs, a toilet was also included in the arrangements for the dead. In others, pits and hidden rooms were built to deter thieves.

ALIGNING THE TEMPLE
Once priests had found a suitable alignment for a temple in accordance with the stars, they buried ritual tools and charms at the four corners of the site.

The hoard of mummies found in Deir el-Bahri contained not only the corpse of Ahmose but also that of Amenhotep I, his son and successor. Amenhotep is best remembered for his great building works. He opened up mines and quarries to extract the raw materials for his temples and monuments, statues and chapels. Turquoise and alabaster, limestone and granite were brought to Thebes from the outermost limits of Egypt.

Amenhotep may have built some of his temples with the aim of observing the stars. To the Egyptians, the cycles of the moon and the movement of the stars and other heavenly bodies were determined by the gods. Often, priests were mathematicians and astronomers, too, concerned with drawing up detailed astronomical charts. Many of

STARGATE
In one pattern of stars, the Egyptians saw the shapes of these animals. They were painted above the coffin of Seti I to help him ascend to the stars.

the great monuments of Egypt were laid out in accordance with the position of the stars. In one burial chamber within the Valley of the Kings, constellations (patterns of stars seen from Earth) are displayed as gods and mythological creatures. The Egyptian constellations were different from ours—for example, the Egyptians represented one constellation as a female hippopotamus with a crocodile on her back. There were many such "astronomical ceilings" designed both to celebrate and to maintain the working of the cosmos. The priests of Egypt also recognized the movements of the five nearest planets (Mercury, Venus, Mars, Jupiter, and Saturn), and connected them with the vast magical power of the universe itself.

In particular, Amenhotep contributed to the building of the monumental sacred site of Karnak, just outside Thebes. Karnak is still one of the wonders of the world, a vast complex of temples and monuments and processional avenues built over many generations and many dynasties. It was a temple city, and at the height of its power and influence had a resident population of more than 80,000.

A processional avenue of colossal sphinxes led from the bank of the Nile to the first "pylon" (a Greek word meaning "gate"), which was entered by a great wooden door. It must have been the most glorious thoroughfare in the world. Inside the first pylon lay a forecourt with shrines and two rows of columns that led to colossal statues. Then another pylon led into a hall with seven rows of nine columns covered in inscriptions and shaped to resemble bundles of papyrus.

EVOLVING TEMPLE
Stone pylons (gateways) still guard each entrance into the sprawling complex of Karnak. From its modest 11th-Dynasty beginnings, pharaoh after pharaoh added to the site, seeking to leave their mark on Egypt's greatest temple. At the heart of the temple's endless halls, courts, and avenues stands the shrine of alabaster that housed the cult statue of Amun-Ra himself.

The great complex at Karnak contained obelisks and sacrificial rooms, sphinxes and colossi, seated pharaohs in divine majesty and processional figures of priests and gods. It was a labyrinth of stone, a sacred city enclosed by a great wall and designed to endure for thousands upon thousands of years. It stands today as a relic and memorial of the hopes and dreams of the ancient past.

The reign of Amenhotep I lasted for 21 years (1525–1504 BCE). It was a time of stability, order, and growing prosperity. He established

Karnak: Temple of Amun

Egyptian temples were not meeting places for worshipers, like churches or mosques are today, but were meant to be real, earthly homes for the gods. The temple of a major god, such as Amun at Karnak (*below*), would expand over time to become a huge complex of offices, schools, libraries, and workshops. Ordinary people were allowed into the outer courtyards, but only priests could enter the heart of the temple itself. Three times a day they walked in procession to the darkest, most holy room where the god lived. There they washed the god's statue and left gifts of food and incense. Through these acts, they hoped to protect the pharaoh and the people.

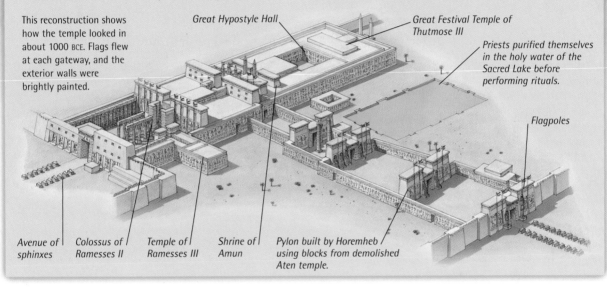

This reconstruction shows how the temple looked in about 1000 BCE. Flags flew at each gateway, and the exterior walls were brightly painted.

Great Hypostyle Hall

Great Festival Temple of Thutmose III

Priests purified themselves in the holy water of the Sacred Lake before performing rituals.

Flagpoles

Avenue of sphinxes

Colossus of Ramesses II

Temple of Ramesses III

Shrine of Amun

Pylon built by Horemheb using blocks from demolished Aten temple.

Thebes, with its major shrines at Karnak, as the center of royal power in Egypt, and set the scene for the expansion of Egypt's boundaries under the later pharaohs of the 18th Dynasty. It was the beginning of Egypt's age of conquests. So famous were Amenhotep's achievements, in fact, that for centuries after his death he was worshiped as a god in and around Thebes. There were festivals in

Amenhotep's honor, and one of the months of the year was named after him. He was worshiped, too, in the village of Deir el-Medina, close to the Valley of the Kings, where archaeologists have found religious statues dedicated to him.

Deir el-Medina is important for other reasons, too, because it gives us a very clear

VILLAGE SECRETS
This is the site of Deir el-Medina. The tomb-workers' village was locked at night to keep the secrets of the tombs from outsiders.

EVERYDAY LIFE
The mud-brick homes of laborers were often crammed together in a maze of alleyways. While the men went off to work in fields or quarries, the women remained at home to bake bread and brew beer. Children played games in the streets.

picture of what daily life was like in Egypt during the New Kingdom. This village had housed the valley's tomb-builders and their families. It was preserved beneath the desert sands for 3,500 years until archaeologists uncovered its intact outlines.

The village, consisting of one main street with other streets leading off, was regular in plan. It contained some 70 identical houses built like little rectangular boxes. Workers' houses in Egypt had an entrance hall, a living and sleeping area, and a kitchen at the back. There was normally a stairway to the flat roof, which in Egypt's hot and sunny climate was used as an extension of the house. Senior officials, of course, lived in much larger accommodations—often in villas with enclosing walls.

The furniture of Egyptian houses was mostly very simple. There were rush mats on the floor, which could also be used as mattresses. The whitewashed walls were decorated with painted linen cloths or hangings. There were chairs as well as beds and small tables. The beds stood on supports to protect sleepers from the creeping creatures of the desert night. Small statues of the gods and of dead members of the family were placed in alcoves or niches. Some houses even had "mummy cupboards"—upright coffins that contained a mummy. The dead person's features were painted onto the coffin so that the living members of the family might look at his or her face. To us, it may seem gruesome, but it shows how closely the Egyptians believed themselves to remain in touch with the dead.

We can also get a good idea of daily life in Egypt from pictures in wall paintings, in tomb art, and on papyrus scrolls. For example, one wall painting shows carpenters at work, sawing planks and smoothing down

BES, THE JOLLY DEVIL
Bes was a household god who protected children. Images of this laughing dwarf were often carved on beds and chairs to ward off evil spirits.

CARPENTERS' SHOP
This highly detailed tomb model shows carpenters at work. The model-maker has even provided spare tools inside the white chest.

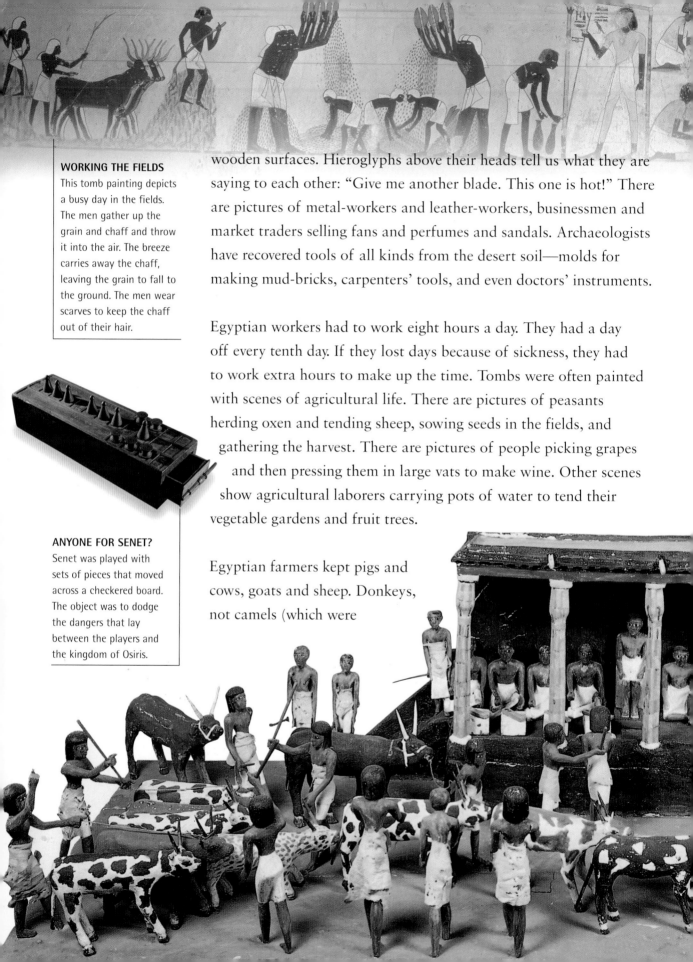

WORKING THE FIELDS
This tomb painting depicts a busy day in the fields. The men gather up the grain and chaff and throw it into the air. The breeze carries away the chaff, leaving the grain to fall to the ground. The men wear scarves to keep the chaff out of their hair.

ANYONE FOR SENET?
Senet was played with sets of pieces that moved across a checkered board. The object was to dodge the dangers that lay between the players and the kingdom of Osiris.

wooden surfaces. Hieroglyphs above their heads tell us what they are saying to each other: "Give me another blade. This one is hot!" There are pictures of metal-workers and leather-workers, businessmen and market traders selling fans and perfumes and sandals. Archaeologists have recovered tools of all kinds from the desert soil—molds for making mud-bricks, carpenters' tools, and even doctors' instruments.

Egyptian workers had to work eight hours a day. They had a day off every tenth day. If they lost days because of sickness, they had to work extra hours to make up the time. Tombs were often painted with scenes of agricultural life. There are pictures of peasants herding oxen and tending sheep, sowing seeds in the fields, and gathering the harvest. There are pictures of people picking grapes and then pressing them in large vats to make wine. Other scenes show agricultural laborers carrying pots of water to tend their vegetable gardens and fruit trees.

Egyptian farmers kept pigs and cows, goats and sheep. Donkeys, not camels (which were unknown in Egypt at the time), were the main beasts of burden. Poultry farmers kept geese and ducks, swans and pigeons. There was a flourishing trade in honey collected from beehives. All farming was carried out under the watchful eye of administrators who decided what should be grown, and how much, and made sure that the pharaoh got his rightful share of the produce.

But images of Egyptian life are not all about work. There are pictures of wrestlers and dancers and acrobats. There are also pictures of people playing senet, a very popular board game in which the players attempted to reach the kingdom of Osiris. Other scenes show people spear-fishing or hippo-hunting in the Nile marshes. Both of these pursuits no doubt combined business with pleasure, hunting for food with sport.

Fish, of course, was part of the normal Egyptian

Buying and selling

The world of Egyptian trade was very different from our own. Since money did not exist, people bought and sold goods by means of barter. Sandals might be purchased with sacks of grain, for example, and perfumes exchanged for pottery. In theory, if a farmer or worker produced more goods than he could use himself, the extra (or surplus) belonged to the pharaoh.

4 sacks of barley   1½ sacks of wheat   = 1 month's salary

¼ deben   7 deben

Rate of exchange

Workers were paid with grain and other basic staples such as meat or beer. The payment for one month's work was four sacks of barley and one-and-a-half sacks of emmer, a type of wheat. The price of goods was calculated using a measure of value called a "deben." A chicken was worth one-quarter of a deben, for example, while a pig was worth seven deben. The amount of grain paid to a laborer amounted to seven deben. In other words, a pig was worth a month's salary.

COUNTING THE CATTLE

This model came from the tomb of Meketra, a wealthy cattle-owner. His cows and oxen are being driven past a team of administrators, who are calculating the royal tax to be paid on each animal. Meketra stands in the center of the dais.

diet. It was eaten with bread, which was baked in molds so that it came out as thick and as doughy as cake. The bread often contained grit that got into the flour when it was ground, and as a result many Egyptians had damaged teeth. Vegetables such as beans and onions were very common, as was meat such as goat or pork. Wine and beef were luxuries found only in wealthy households, but beer was common and drunk by adults and children alike. It was a strange kind of beer, however, brewed from barley bread, dates, and water. It was nutritious and thick, almost like a soup, and not very alcoholic.

Today, we would say that the Egyptians had a healthy diet (except, perhaps, for the gritty bread). However, X-ray examination of mummies shows that many Egyptians suffered from arthritis and back problems. The unending labor of daily life, the lifting and carrying of heavy weights, injured their bodies. The water from the Nile itself often gave people intestinal worms and diseases. Eye infections and cataracts were a problem. The Egyptians consulted doctors who prescribed a range of magical and practical remedies, including the use of medicinal herbs. They also recommended praying to the gods.

The Egyptians were also very clean. Ordinary people bathed in the Nile, while the better-off had water in their

MEALTIME
Egyptians ate their meals with their fingers. Meat was cooked with imported herbs and spices. Vegetables were mashed, fried, and washed down with beer, of which there was several varieties.

DRESSING UP
Wealthy Egyptians took a great deal of trouble over their appearance. Both sexes wore wigs over their short hair, and women attached scented cones of animal fat to their heads. Makeup, jewelry, and fine linens completed the look.

SIDELOCK OF YOUTH
Here, a young prince wears his sidelock in a gold clasp. Sometimes, children's sidelocks were platted into an "S" shape, representing the hieroglyph for "youth."

bathrooms. They used soap as well as pills that cleansed the breath. They rubbed their bodies with aromatic oils and perfumes, so that they must have been a sweet-smelling people.

Wealthy Egyptians—both men and women—wore wigs and makeup. They made eye paint from minerals, which they ground up on palettes of slate and mixed with animal fats. They used rouge on their cheeks and painted their lips red. The wealthy also loved the glint of gold above all things, and adorned themselves with collars and bracelets of gold decorated with semiprecious stones.

But no description of the Egyptians would be complete without mentioning the religious rituals that were part of everyday life. For example, all children wore a long piece of hair, known as "the sidelock of youth," on the right side of the head. When a boy was considered to have become a man, a ceremony was held to cut off the sidelock. People made daily offerings of food and drink to the household gods in their homes. They wrote letters to the dead and placed them in the shrines of their ancestors.

The Egyptians were a deeply spiritual people who believed that they lived in close communion with the dead and with the gods. Small wonder that religious ceremonies accompanied almost every aspect of existence in Egypt, from birth to death.

COSMETICS
From malachite, a copper ore, the Egyptians made green eye paint to symbolize fertility. Eyeliner was made from lead ore. They applied it by looking in mirrors of polished bronze, like this one.

EVERYDAY GODS
Some gods gave comfort in times of trouble. For example, pregnant women prayed to Taweret, shown here as a pregnant hippo, when they were giving birth.

ANIMAL OFFERINGS
The Egyptians often made offerings of animal mummies. Excavators have found vast cemeteries of mummified cats, ibises, and baboons.

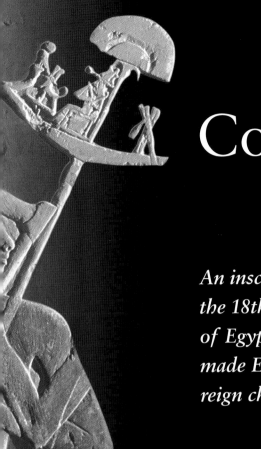

CHAPTER SIX

Conquest *and* glory

An inscription of Thutmose I, the third pharaoh of the 18th Dynasty, declares: "I made the boundaries of Egypt as far as that which the sun encircles. I made Egypt the superior of every land." His brief reign changed the map of Egypt for centuries.

PHARAOHS WERE IN FACT typically boastful about their achievements. Thutmose I had good reason to be proud of his victories, however. During his six-year reign, he greatly extended Egypt's power and fame. He led an army into Palestine and Syria, and also crushed the power of Nubia to the south of Egypt, sailing farther up the Nile than any pharaoh had ever done before. He returned with the corpse of a defeated Nubian leader hanging from the prow of his ship. The victorious pharaoh set up buildings and had inscriptions carved everywhere, especially in the conquered kingdom of Nubia, and he added new gates and courtyards to the complex of buildings at Karnak.

His successor, Thutmose II, reigned for 14 years, but seems to have been in poor health for much of this time. His influence on Egyptian history was really the result of

◀ Carved relief depicting Queen Hatshepsut's expedition to Punt

his marriage to his half-sister Hatshepsut, the daughter of Thutmose I. Hatshepsut was one of the most formidable figures of the 18th Dynasty. When her husband died in about 1479 BCE, she acted as regent for her stepson, the infant Thutmose III, and ambitiously set out to rule Egypt in the manner of a pharaoh. Her position of power lasted for more than 20 years.

Hatshepsut embarked upon a huge building program. She built a palace for herself at Karnak, and erected two great obelisks of red granite there, which had to be floated up the Nile on rafts. She prepared a great tomb for herself in the Valley of the Kings. She constructed a mighty temple at Deir el-Bahri close to the site of Mentuhotep's temple of 500 years before. Her temple, known as the "Holy of Holies," was built into the face of a cliff in a series of terraces. A long row of columns fronted the entrance to the temple, and above them stood a line of colossal statues of Osiris. In the temple itself, carvings and inscriptions commemorated the events and exploits of her reign.

Hatshepsut was the most powerful woman in the world, and one of her titles was "foremost of women." In some symbolic images of her, she is even portrayed wearing the false beard of the pharaoh. In others, she is a sphinx with a lion's mane. She demanded wealth and

FEMALE KING

Hatshepsut legitimized her rule with propaganda. She had reliefs carved in which the god Amun impregnates her mother, to suggest that Hatshepsut was divine.

TEMPLE OF GENIUS

Hatshepsut's temple was designed by a genius architect named Senenmut. The colonnaded terraces rising to a central sanctuary are unique in Egyptian architecture.

tribute from all corners of Egypt. Gold and stone, precious jewels and precious woods flowed into her treasury. One picture shows whole incense trees brought in baskets from the southern kingdom of Punt to be planted in front of her temple.

But Hatshepsut's power only lasted while Thutmose III remained too young to govern. It is possible that she managed to keep him under her control until the end of her life, but it became clear that the young pharaoh resented his stepmother's rule, and may even have arranged for her to be murdered. Even if he did not kill her, he went to great lengths to erase all records of her rule over Egypt after her death. He smashed her statues and covered up her monuments. He vandalized her temple at Deir el-Bahri, and destroyed her sanctuary at Karnak. It is as if he wished to take her name out of history altogether.

After years of being overshadowed by his stepmother, Thutmose III lost no time in establishing his own fame as a military leader and a great pharaoh. He need not have worried about his reputation,

THE GREAT EXPEDITION
A scene carved on a colonnade of Hatshepsut's temple records her famous trading expedition to Punt. Here, the traders are greeted by Eti, the enormously fat Queen of Punt, who stands next to her elderly, skinny husband. The pair may have been carved for comic effect.

VALLEY VIEW
The dramatic setting of Hatshepsut's temple, nestling in the Theban hills, can be seen best from the air. Directly behind the cliff lies the Valley of the Kings.

however, since he had all the qualities of a truly brilliant statesman. He excelled at administration, and encouraged the arts. He was an accomplished horseman and athlete. As a general, he expanded Egypt's empire to its greatest extent, fighting many campaigns in Palestine and Syria, which at this time were divided into small kingdoms and city-states. Thutmose conquered some 350 cities in the region, and had the excellent idea of bringing back the captured sons of foreign rulers to be educated in Egypt. When they returned to their own lands, they no longer regarded Egypt as an enemy and helped to pass on Egyptian civilization. Thutmose also married a number of Syrian princesses, as a way of gaining political influence in the region, and these young brides became part of his extensive harem.

Thutmose III was a national hero whose 54-year reign had an enormous impact on Egyptian history. His name was still held in awe a thousand years after his death, in the dying days of ancient Egyptian civilization. In addition to his spectacular military victories,

SPLENDID KING
This fine fragment shows Thutmose III resplendent in the feathered "Atef" crown. Egyptian pharaohs had up to 100 different crowns for every type of religious and state occasion.

The Battle of Megiddo

Early in his reign, Thutmose III faced a rebellion by the princes of Kadesh and Megiddo, who were refusing to pay tribute to Egypt. Undaunted, Thutmose mobilized his army to take Megiddo (a city in northern Israel). There were three routes to the city: two easy roads, and one mountain path through the Aruna Pass. The king's generals advised an easy route, since the pass was open to ambush. But Thutmose knew that his enemies would expect him on the easy roads, and, convinced that the god Amun-Ra was with him, led his troops single-file through the pass. The gamble paid off. He emerged unexpectedly between the princes' northern and southern forces and routed them in a battle the next day. The enemy fled in disarray to the city, which surrendered after a seven-month siege.

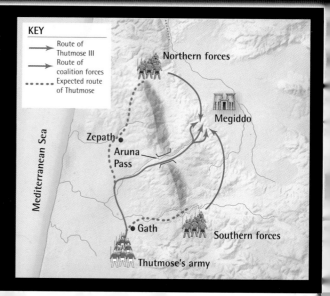

KEY
Route of Thutmose III
Route of coalition forces
Expected route of Thutmose

Northern forces
Megiddo
Zepath
Aruna Pass
Mediterranean Sea
Gath
Southern forces
Thutmose's army

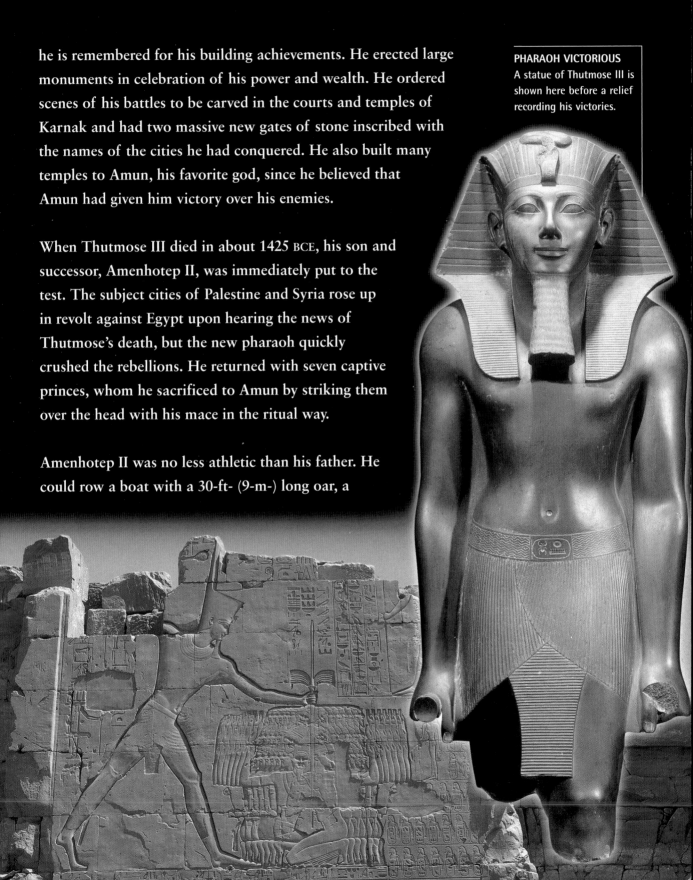

he is remembered for his building achievements. He erected large monuments in celebration of his power and wealth. He ordered scenes of his battles to be carved in the courts and temples of Karnak and had two massive new gates of stone inscribed with the names of the cities he had conquered. He also built many temples to Amun, his favorite god, since he believed that Amun had given him victory over his enemies.

When Thutmose III died in about 1425 BCE, his son and successor, Amenhotep II, was immediately put to the test. The subject cities of Palestine and Syria rose up in revolt against Egypt upon hearing the news of Thutmose's death, but the new pharaoh quickly crushed the rebellions. He returned with seven captive princes, whom he sacrificed to Amun by striking them over the head with his mace in the ritual way.

Amenhotep II was no less athletic than his father. He could row a boat with a 30-ft- (9-m-) long oar, a

PHARAOH VICTORIOUS
A statue of Thutmose III is shown here before a relief recording his victories.

considerable feat of strength. There is even an image of him shooting arrows from a fast-moving chariot. Amenhotep's longbow was buried with him, but although he is one of the few kings whose mummy was found still inside its sarcophagus, the bow had been stolen.

Amenhotep II had at least ten sons from a large number of royal wives. Perhaps not surprisingly, the sons fought among themselves for the throne after his death. Thutmose IV emerged as the winner, probably because he was the boldest and most ruthless of the bunch, or else had gained the most support from the palace priests. Thutmose IV himself claimed that none other than the Great Sphinx had chosen him. After falling asleep in the Sphinx's shadow one day, he dreamed he heard Ra's voice speaking through the statue's stone mouth. The god declared that Thutmose would become pharaoh on condition that he restored the Sphinx to its original glory. Thutmose did as the god asked, and won the crown of Egypt.

Thutmose IV was also an unusually energetic ruler. He restored the strength of the royal bureaucracy and kept the country's border defenses in order. He built monuments to himself all over the country, and went to great lengths in his inscriptions to proclaim his kingship and divinity— perhaps because he was not the direct heir and needed to justify his rule.

SUN WORSHIPERS

The sun was worshiped in a variety of forms during the New Kingdom. Just as Amun was joined with the sun god, Ra, to become Amun-Ra, so was Egypt's other principal god, Horus, who became Ra-Harakhty, a falcon with a sun-disc on its head.

BURIED IN SAND

Drifting sands have buried the Great Sphinx up to the neck for most of its 4,500-year history. Thutmose IV made the first attempt to free the sculpture in about 1400 BCE. A further effort was made in 1818 CE, but it was only in 1925 CE that the Sphinx was finally dug out.

RIDDLE OF THE SPHINX

Thutmose IV is shown here making offerings of sacred ointments. His claim to have been chosen by the Great Sphinx was obviously a story designed to strengthen his title to the throne.

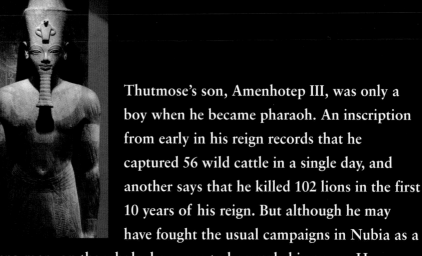

CULT FOLLOWING
This awesome pink quartzite statue of Amenhotep III was found buried, undamaged, at Luxor Temple, Thebes, in 1989. The fine quality of the carving and the king's idealized, youthful face suggest that this was a cult statue.

Thutmose's son, Amenhotep III, was only a boy when he became pharaoh. An inscription from early in his reign records that he captured 56 wild cattle in a single day, and another says that he killed 102 lions in the first 10 years of his reign. But although he may have fought the usual campaigns in Nubia as a young man, on the whole, he seems to have ruled in peace. He exchanged friendly letters with neighboring kings. For example, the king of Assyria in Mesopotamia wrote to him asking for gold to decorate the new palace that he was building. "Gold in your country is as common as dust," the Assyrian king told him. The king of the Mitanni, another Middle-Eastern power, offered his daughter to Amenhotep in exchange for piles of gold.

During Amenhotep III's 38-year reign, Egypt enjoyed an unparalleled economic boom. Riches poured into the kingdom not from military conquests but through foreign trade.
Such prosperity encouraged a great

PEACEFUL PHARAOH
Although he was depicted in the traditional way as a warrior king, Amenhotep III reigned in peace.

nourishing of art and architecture. It is a measure of the pharaoh's wealth that he built monuments on a vast scale, including an opulent new palace called "the House of Joy." Beside it was a pleasure lake, created especially for his favorite wife, Queen Tiy. The king and queen celebrated the opening of the lake by sailing on it in the royal barge. The couple lived in extravagant luxury, enjoying all the delights of palace life. The evidence of Amenhotep's mummy seems

to confirm his fondness for fine living. It tells us that he had grown fat and must have suffered agonies from tooth decay.

Amenhotep III built temples all over Egypt, including one to Sobek, the crocodile god whose cult center was at Crocodilopolis, meaning "Crocodile City." He rebuilt parts of Karnak, and had colossal statues of animal deities erected in his funerary temples. The pharaoh shrewdly encouraged these other cults as a way of reducing the growing power of the priests of Amun. One new cult worshiped a strange form of the god Ra known as the "Aten." This, as we will see, was soon to have far-reaching consequences for Egypt.

But perhaps Amenhotep's most famous memorials are the Colossi of Memnon, two gigantic statues of the

HALLS OF THE GODS
This image shows how the Colonnade Hall of
Amenhotep III at Luxor Temple, Thebes, may
have looked upon completion in about 1355 BCE.

seated pharaoh placed at the entrance of his
mortuary temple. Each one is 60 ft (18 m)
high. As the statues aged, one of them gave
off a sound like a low moan, usually in the
morning. Greek travelers to the site believed it was King Memnon,
calling to the goddess of the dawn, which is how the statues got their
present name. The temple guarded by these two massive stone figures
contained many great courtyards, with pillars rising 40 ft (12 m) into
the air. Surrounding the complex was a wall no less than 25 ft (7.5 m)
thick. Inside the temple itself were 36 further statues of Amenhotep.

COLOSSI OF MEMNON
The strange sound
emitted by one of the
statues was probably an
effect of temperature
change on the stone at
dawn and at dusk. The
temple guarded by the
colossi was quarried by
later pharaohs, who
plundered it for its stone.

Egyptian statuary is rightly praised as being among the most
profound and beautiful ever produced in the world. Not all
Egyptian statues were on the gigantic scale of
those made for Amenhotep III. Many of them
were life-size. Human figures in statues—
whether of gods or pharaohs, priests or
nobles—are always shown in standard
poses that were already established by the
time of the Old Kingdom. The motionless
figures face straight ahead with squared
shoulders. They hold their arms close to
their sides, with clenched fists if empty-
handed, or cross them over their chests. In
standing statues, the figure is erect and alert, eyes
focused ahead, left foot forward. Some statues
kneel to make offerings. Scribes squat cross-
legged with a papyrus scroll across their lap.

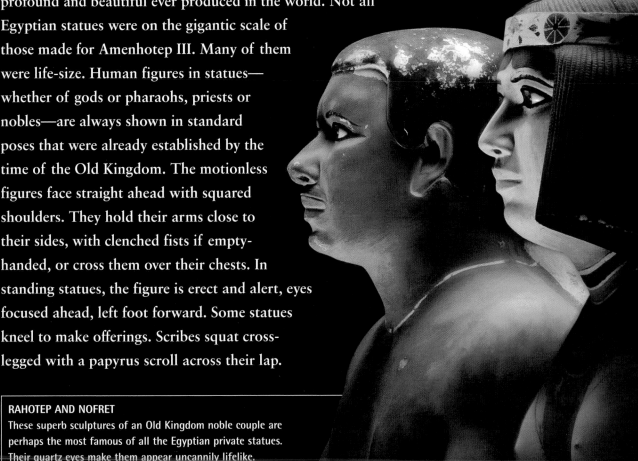

RAHOTEP AND NOFRET
These superb sculptures of an Old Kingdom noble couple are
perhaps the most famous of all the Egyptian private statues.
Their quartz eyes make them appear uncannily lifelike.

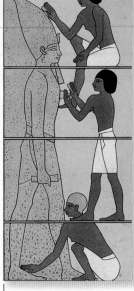

There were also "private statues", generally of family groups—mother and son, or husband and wife. The man often sits, with the woman standing beside him. She may have her arm around the man, as a gesture of possessiveness or of affection. Sometimes the couple is holding hands. The figures often differ in size and scale to denote differences in the rank or status of the people shown.

COLOSSAL WORK
Sculptors worked on large statues by erecting a light scaffolding of poles and platforms tied with rope.

The expressions on the faces of Egyptian statues are always serene and calm, caught at a moment when youth turns to adulthood. The figures gaze into the far distance, as if they are above the concerns of the world. Some of them have a faint smile. Only in late Egyptian art do we begin to see the beginnings of individual portraiture, although during the reign of Amenhotep III, a new, more realistic style was set.

HEAD OF AMENHOTEP III
To carve works such as this pink granite head, masons first pounded the block with hard rocks. Sculptors then chiseled out the features. Finally, the surface was polished with flat stones.

Painting in Egypt also tended to be very formal. In tombs and temples, the wall

Divine proportions

Egyptian artists and sculptors followed a fixed system of proportion. They began by drawing a grid of horizontal and vertical lines (*right*) to calculate what they called "divine proportions." The vertical axis, for the upright human figure, had seven horizontal lines to mark the proportions of different parts of the body. Artists then sketched in figures and objects. Master designers checked and made corrections before work began.

Examples of unfinished art reveal the artists' methods

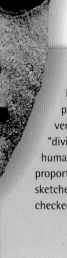

paintings moved in horizontal lines from top to bottom. The earliest events happen at the top, and the later ones at the bottom. For most of the Egyptian period, artists did not attempt to give an idea of perspective (showing objects at different sizes depending on their distance from the viewer). In paintings, the limbs and the full torso of each figure are always depicted, but the face is always shown in profile. It is in that sense a very conventional if very beautiful art. Outdoor and indoor scenes are very stylized, so that, for example, a tree may represent a garden.

The images were sometimes carved on the walls of the tomb and the temple before they were painted. More frequently, however, the wall was rubbed smooth and flat with stones before being covered with white plaster to form a prepared surface to take the paint. The best artists worked freehand—that is, they painted directly onto the wall with their brushes without the aid of preliminary sketches and drawings. Less talented artists were employed to decorate the darker areas of a tomb, or to paint unimportant tombs.

Egypt was at the height of its magnificence during the reign of Amenhotep III. Never had the country been richer or more powerful. It was a period of abundant harvests and booming foreign trade. Precious metals and precious stones poured into the state treasuries, and Egypt's artistic achievements reached new standards of excellence. But this prosperous and happy world was soon to be turned upside down. By a quirk of fate, Amenhotep's eldest son, Prince Thutmose, died. The succession then passed a younger brother, who proved to be the most controversial ruler in Egyptian history.

Grinder for crushing pigments

PAINT PALETTE
Artists used stone palettes like this one to mix colored pigments. Black could be produced from charcoal or soot. Red came from ocher, and blue and green from minerals.

UNFOLDING STORY
This painting of a midwife delivering a baby is typical of the way in which Egyptian art depicts a story unfolding from left to right, rather like a comic strip.

CHAPTER SEVEN

The *religious* revolution

With the death of Amenhotep III, there began one of the strangest episodes in Egyptian history. In one stroke, Amenhotep's successor swept away the old and familiar gods who had watched over Egypt for more than 2,000 years.

I N THEIR PLACE, he set up a new state religion: the worship of the Aten. This deity was always portrayed as a sun-disc with great rays reaching downward and ending in outstretched hands.

The new pharaoh was crowned Amenhotep IV, but soon changed his name to Akhenaten, which means, literally, "servant of the Aten."

He also called himself "the dazzling Aten," a name that suggests he identified himself so closely with the Aten that god and pharaoh were one and the same. The cult of the Aten already existed in Egypt as part of the worship of the sun god, Ra, but Akhenaten took the astonishing step of making the Aten Egypt's sole god.

The Aten represented life and energy. It was the creative source of the world. At Akhenaten's command, the temples of all other gods were closed down or converted to

◀ Tutankhamun is anointed by his wife, Ankhesenamun

the worship of the Aten. The old religious festivals were abolished. The ancient cults were banned. The names of earlier deities were chiseled away from walls and obelisks. Some historians have suggested that Akhenaten made these sweeping changes in order to destroy the power of the priests of Amun, who had become too rich and important in Egyptian society. But there is no firm evidence for this. Others think that Akhenaten was obsessed and mad, a visionary and a mystic, but again, we cannot be sure what really motivated him.

Of course, even the greatest pharaoh could not have carried out such radical policies all by himself. Historians believe that Akhenaten must have had the active cooperation of the army. To describe the overturning of the old religion as a revolution is no less than the truth. In a society where life revolved around the worship of the gods, people must have thought that the world as they knew it had ended.

Akhenaten built a new city in honor of his god on an uninhabited site said to have

THE DAZZLING ATEN
In this typical example of Amarna art, Akhenaten is making offerings to the Aten. The god's rays end in small hands, one of which is touching the king's face with an ankh, the symbol of life.

SACRED CITY OF AMARNA
This model shows how the principal buildings of Amarna may have looked. A jetty led from the Nile to the royal palace, behind which stood the open-air Great Aten Temple.

been chosen by divine inspiration. He called it Akhetaten, or "horizon of the Aten," perhaps because the outline of the valley at this point resembled the hieroglyph for "horizon." Akhetaten stretched for 8 miles (12 km) along the east bank of the Nile. We know the site by its modern Egyptian name, el-Amarna, or, more simply, Amarna.

Amarna was not laid out in the usual style of Egyptian cities, on a grid pattern of crossing streets, but took the form of a number of villages grouped together. There was a workmen's village for those building the temple and burial chambers, as well as areas for workshops and sculptors' studios. This may have been the pharaoh's own plan, and he may have designed the layout of the temples and the royal palaces as well, which suggests that he had thought very deeply about the new way of life he wished to create.

THE FACE OF A VISIONARY
Akhenaten chose to be portrayed in a style that was very different from the usual idealized images of pharaohs. His face has small slanting eyes, a very long, narrow nose, a full, prominent mouth, and an exaggerated, rounded chin.

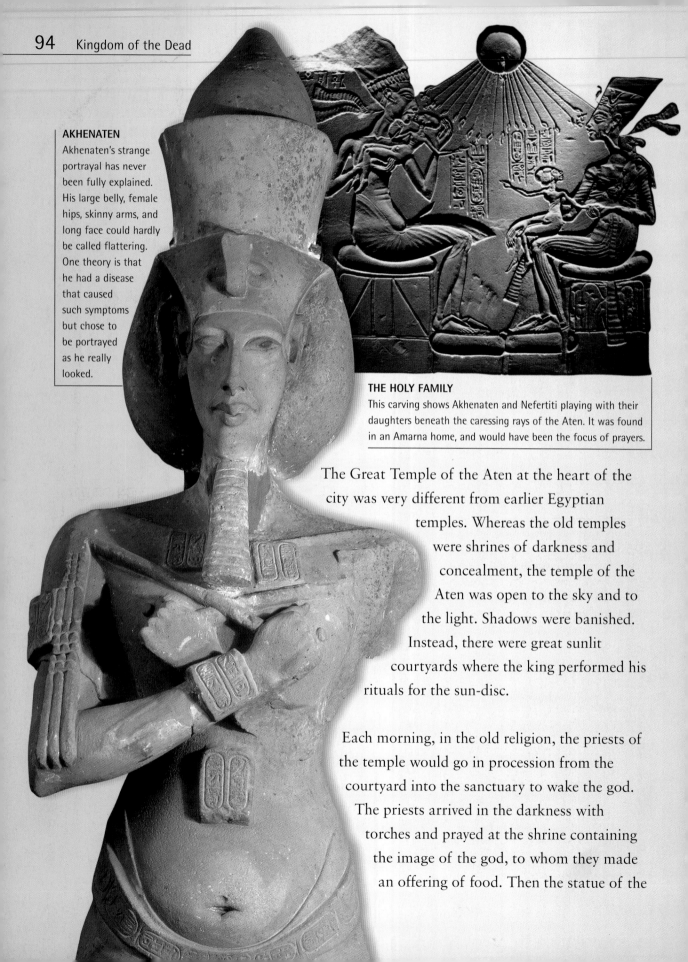

AKHENATEN
Akhenaten's strange portrayal has never been fully explained. His large belly, female hips, skinny arms, and long face could hardly be called flattering. One theory is that he had a disease that caused such symptoms but chose to be portrayed as he really looked.

THE HOLY FAMILY
This carving shows Akhenaten and Nefertiti playing with their daughters beneath the caressing rays of the Aten. It was found in an Amarna home, and would have been the focus of prayers.

The Great Temple of the Aten at the heart of the city was very different from earlier Egyptian temples. Whereas the old temples were shrines of darkness and concealment, the temple of the Aten was open to the sky and to the light. Shadows were banished. Instead, there were great sunlit courtyards where the king performed his rituals for the sun-disc.

Each morning, in the old religion, the priests of the temple would go in procession from the courtyard into the sanctuary to wake the god. The priests arrived in the darkness with torches and prayed at the shrine containing the image of the god, to whom they made an offering of food. Then the statue of the god was taken from the shrine, and cleaned and anointed before being put back. As the priests left the sanctuary, a servant swept the floor to remove all traces of their footprints. The priests' torches were extinguished before they proceeded back into the light. The temple was a well-run machine dedicated to the worship of the god and to preserving the harmony and order of the cosmos. All this was abolished by Akhenaten.

The only statues permitted in the Aten temples were those of the pharaoh and his family. The pharaoh was the only representative of the Aten on earth. He was the living form of the god. The pharaoh gave light and life. He intervened directly between the Aten and the rest of humankind. In people's homes, no statues or images of the old household

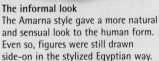

The Amarna style

Akhenaten also changed Egypt's artistic styles. The art of the "Amarna period" is freer, more relaxed, and full of detail; it shows movement and change. It has been described as more realistic than previous art, which was very formal and restrained.

The informal look
The Amarna style gave a more natural and sensual look to the human form. Even so, figures were still drawn side-on in the stylized Egyptian way.

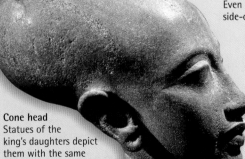

Cone head
Statues of the king's daughters depict them with the same elongated head and pear-shaped body as their father. The reason for this is not known.

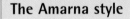

Ornate nature
Amarna artists captured the natural world that thrived beneath the life-giving rays of the Aten. This grape cluster is an example of their craft.

THE PRIESTHOOD
Akhenaten may have hated Egypt's priesthood because of the power it had held over his father. The priests coexisted with the Aten at first, but were soon swept away.

ROLE OF A KING
Nefertiti's powerful status is clear from images that show her taking the king's place in religious rituals.

gods were permitted—only images of the royal family. The courtiers of Akhenaten proclaimed themselves to have been worthless orphans who were saved by the great pharaoh. Temple frescoes were filled with the pharaoh's image. A great processional avenue linked Akhenaten's palaces, and every day he drove his chariot along it in order to display his divinity to his people.

It is difficult to think of another pharaoh who so deliberately molded Egypt in the image of his beliefs. And those beliefs were revolutionary in the extreme. No longer did the dead have to ask Osiris to guide them through the underworld, because it was through the Akhenaten's mercy alone that they would find their way to eternal happiness in the afterlife. The poem known as the Hymn to the Aten, believed to have been written by the pharaoh himself, celebrates these ideas.

Akhenaten was so involved with the new religion that he seems to have left matters of government to his officials. In the 19th century, a fascinating collection of letters addressed to Akhenaten was found at Amarna. Many were from the rulers of the pharaoh's subject cities in Palestine and Syria, usually asking for gold or military aid, and addressed the pharaoh in very respectful terms. One letter begins "my lord, my sun-god, I prostrate myself at the feet of my lord, my sun-god, seven times and seven times." In particular, the letters provide evidence that the pharaoh's inattention was causing Egypt's empire to weaken and unravel.

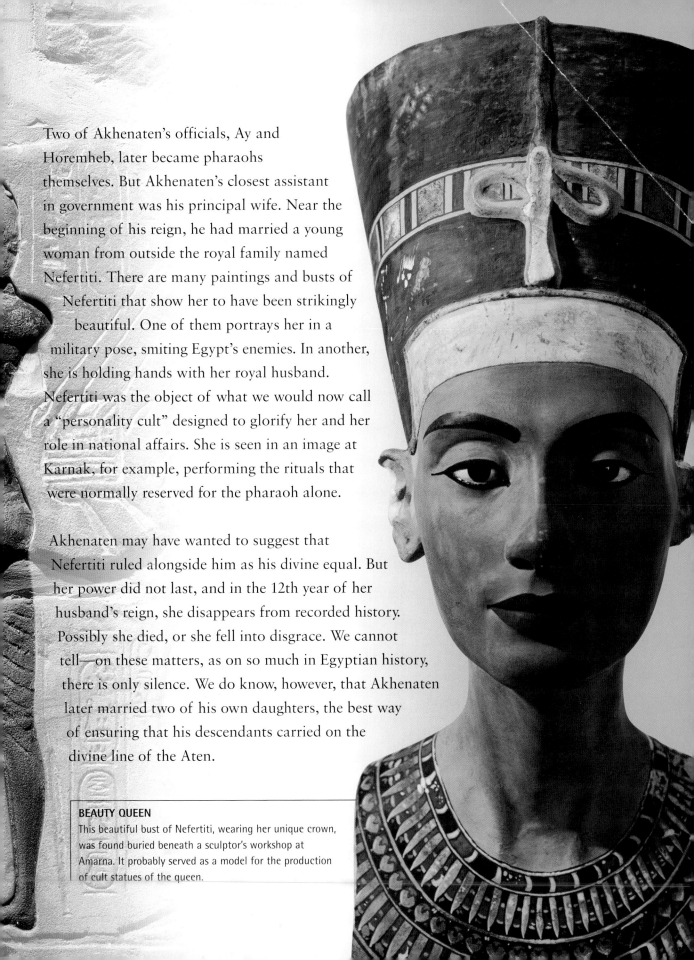

Two of Akhenaten's officials, Ay and
Horemheb, later became pharaohs
themselves. But Akhenaten's closest assistant
in government was his principal wife. Near the
beginning of his reign, he had married a young
woman from outside the royal family named
Nefertiti. There are many paintings and busts of
Nefertiti that show her to have been strikingly
beautiful. One of them portrays her in a
military pose, smiting Egypt's enemies. In another,
she is holding hands with her royal husband.
Nefertiti was the object of what we would now call
a "personality cult" designed to glorify her and her
role in national affairs. She is seen in an image at
Karnak, for example, performing the rituals that
were normally reserved for the pharaoh alone.

Akhenaten may have wanted to suggest that
Nefertiti ruled alongside him as his divine equal. But
her power did not last, and in the 12th year of her
husband's reign, she disappears from recorded history.
Possibly she died, or she fell into disgrace. We cannot
tell—on these matters, as on so much in Egyptian history,
there is only silence. We do know, however, that Akhenaten
later married two of his own daughters, the best way
of ensuring that his descendants carried on the
divine line of the Aten.

BEAUTY QUEEN
This beautiful bust of Nefertiti, wearing her unique crown,
was found buried beneath a sculptor's workshop at
Amarna. It probably served as a model for the production
of cult statues of the queen.

ANKHESENAMUN
This exquisite picture was painted on the lid of a precious chest belonging to Tutankhamun. It shows his queen, Ankhesenamun, in a garden of lotus flowers. Howard Carter, the English archaeologist who discovered it in the king's tomb, labeled it as an "unsigned picture by a great master."

Akhenaten died in the 16th year of his turbulent and unparalleled reign. But his policies did not long survive him. After his death, his religion was proclaimed false, and his name was defaced or removed from thousands of monuments. Even his tomb was vandalized. Almost immediately the old cults and beliefs returned to Egypt.

Akhenaten's short-lived successor, Smenkhkare, is a shadowy figure. Even his identity is in doubt. He was probably a younger brother of Akhenaten, but some believe he may have been a woman—Nefertiti herself ruling under a new name after her husband's death. Whatever his identity, Smenkhkare was succeeded by a king who became the most famous in Egyptian history: the nine-year-old Tutankhamun.

The boy-king inherited a demoralized and stricken kingdom. With the old religion banished by Akhenaten, the temples were disused and the monuments defaced. As a result, according to a stone inscription of Tutankhamun's reign known as the Restoration Stele, the gods had turned their face away from Egypt. They had hardened their hearts against the kingdom.

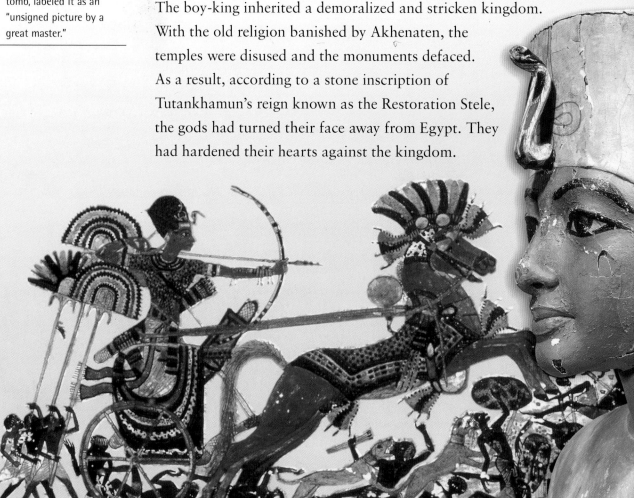

Egypt's army was no longer successful in battle. In the royal palaces there was chaos.

The first act of the boy-king's reign was to abandon Amarna and move the government to Memphis, the ancient capital. Because of Tutankhamun's young age, this decision was probably taken for him by the high officials who surrounded him, in particular Ay and Horemheb. To ensure stability, the young pharaoh was immediately married to Akhenaten's widow, who may also have been Tutankhamun's stepsister. The pharaoh changed his birth name from Tutankhaten to Tutankhamun, symbolizing his return to the old religion and the cult of Amun. We do not know if the priests of Amun had all been killed by Akhenaten, or if they had simply been disbanded, but a new priesthood was created from among the dignitaries of the country.

THE KING'S DUMMY
This wooden "dummy" shows the king as he looked before he died in about 1327 BCE. It was probably dressed in his clothes and jewelry.

SEAT OF POWER
Tutankhamun's superbly crafted throne was found in his tomb. It is richly inlaid with gold, ivory, and various colored woods. The king probably sat on it when giving audiences.

WHEELS OF VICTORY
This painting, drawn in minute detail on the side of Tutankhamun's hunting chest, shows the king riding his chariot over Egypt's traditional enemies, the Syrians and the Nubians. It does not depict a real event, but symbolizes the king's triumph over chaos.

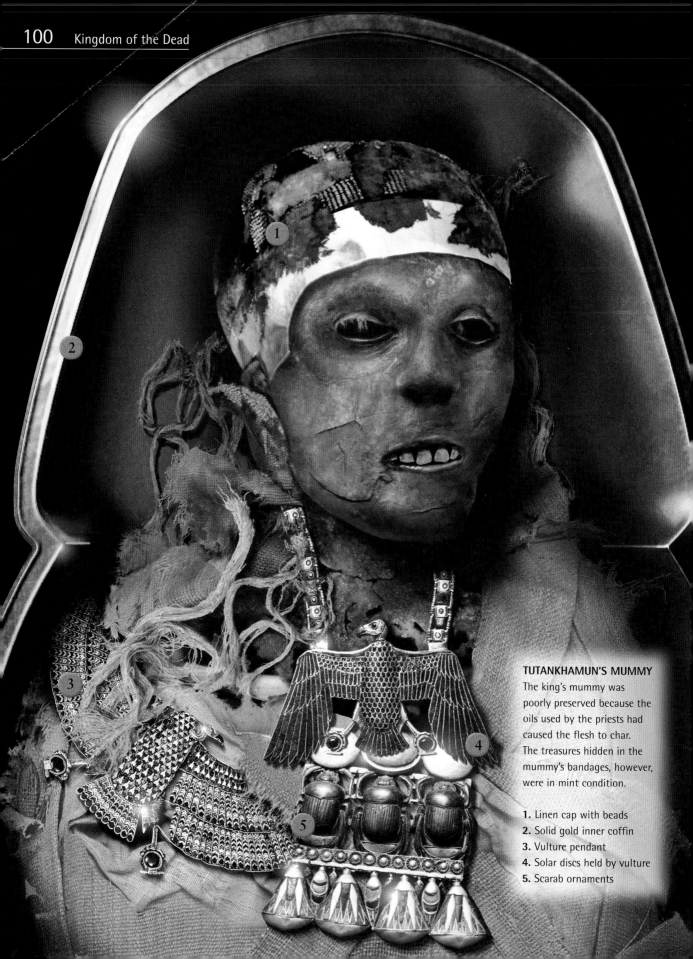

TUTANKHAMUN'S MUMMY
The king's mummy was
poorly preserved because the
oils used by the priests had
caused the flesh to char.
The treasures hidden in the
mummy's bandages, however,
were in mint condition.

1. Linen cap with beads
2. Solid gold inner coffin
3. Vulture pendant
4. Solar discs held by vulture
5. Scarab ornaments

BABY MUMMIES
Two tiny coffins found in the king's tomb each contained a mummified female fetus. They are probably the bodies of Tutankhamun's stillborn daughters.

Ay and Horemheb sent military expeditions to Syria and Palestine, perhaps to emphasize Egypt's renewal of power. Images on a box found in Tutankhamun's tomb show him wielding a bow and arrow in battle, and hunting lions and gazelles. But it is unlikely that Tutankhamun took part in war, and these scenes are intended to glorify his majesty. Images from the tomb of Horemheb may be more accurate—they show the general leading enemy captives before the young pharaoh. The prisoners have ropes around their necks, and their hands are tied.

We know from the evidence of Tutankhamun's mummy that he died at about the age of 17. X-rays taken of his skull reveal a tiny piece of bone lodged within the brain cavity, so it is possible that the pharaoh was killed by a blow to the head or died as the result of an accidental fall. He was buried in some haste, and was taken to a tomb that was originally designed for Ay. By a curious chance of history, however, it is this tomb that has made Tutankhamun immortal. It provides the only evidence ever found of a complete royal burial. It is the jewel within the Valley of the Kings. Since the valley was barren and remote, it was believed that it could easily be protected. In fact, all the tombs were robbed in ancient times.

All, that is, except for the tomb of Tutankhamun. Its eventual discovery in 1922 was one of the most sensational archaeological finds ever made. Two

PROTECTIVE GODDESS
This finely modeled gold figure is one of the four protecting goddesses who stood guard around the king's canopic shrine. The figure is carved in the artistic style of Amarna.

Tutankhamun's burial chamber

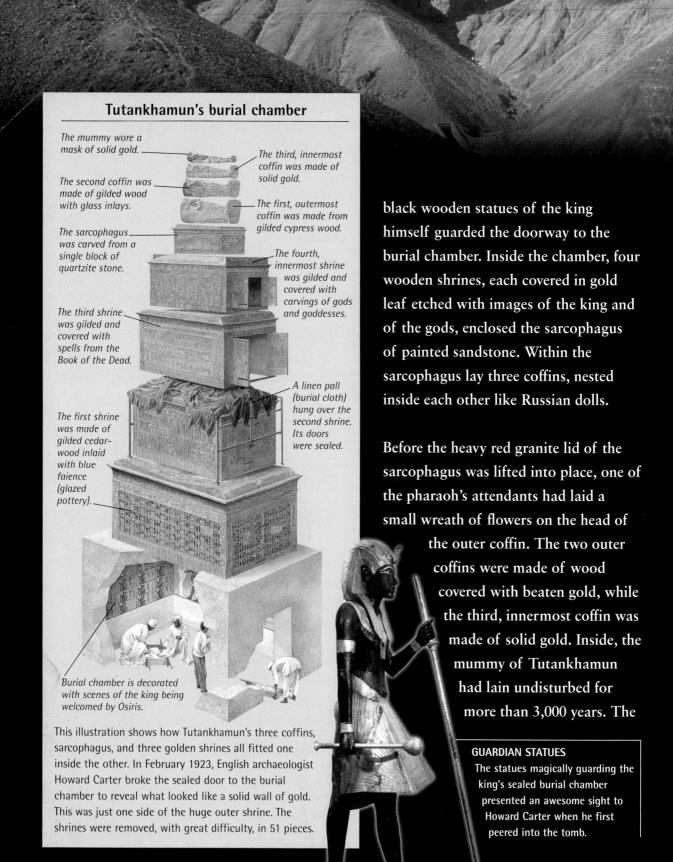

The mummy wore a mask of solid gold.

The third, innermost coffin was made of solid gold.

The second coffin was made of gilded wood with glass inlays.

The first, outermost coffin was made from gilded cypress wood.

The sarcophagus was carved from a single block of quartzite stone.

The fourth, innermost shrine was gilded and covered with carvings of gods and goddesses.

The third shrine was gilded and covered with spells from the Book of the Dead.

A linen pall (burial cloth) hung over the second shrine. Its doors were sealed.

The first shrine was made of gilded cedar-wood inlaid with blue faience (glazed pottery).

Burial chamber is decorated with scenes of the king being welcomed by Osiris.

This illustration shows how Tutankhamun's three coffins, sarcophagus, and three golden shrines all fitted one inside the other. In February 1923, English archaeologist Howard Carter broke the sealed door to the burial chamber to reveal what looked like a solid wall of gold. This was just one side of the huge outer shrine. The shrines were removed, with great difficulty, in 51 pieces.

black wooden statues of the king himself guarded the doorway to the burial chamber. Inside the chamber, four wooden shrines, each covered in gold leaf etched with images of the king and of the gods, enclosed the sarcophagus of painted sandstone. Within the sarcophagus lay three coffins, nested inside each other like Russian dolls.

Before the heavy red granite lid of the sarcophagus was lifted into place, one of the pharaoh's attendants had laid a small wreath of flowers on the head of the outer coffin. The two outer coffins were made of wood covered with beaten gold, while the third, innermost coffin was made of solid gold. Inside, the mummy of Tutankhamun had lain undisturbed for more than 3,000 years. The

GUARDIAN STATUES
The statues magically guarding the king's sealed burial chamber presented an awesome sight to Howard Carter when he first peered into the tomb.

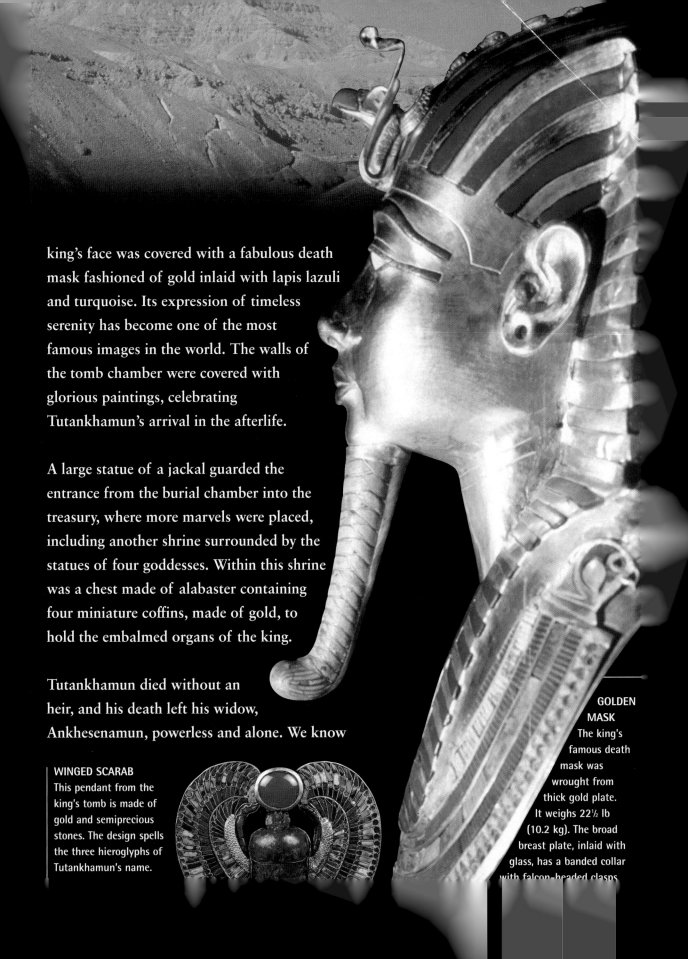

king's face was covered with a fabulous death mask fashioned of gold inlaid with lapis lazuli and turquoise. Its expression of timeless serenity has become one of the most famous images in the world. The walls of the tomb chamber were covered with glorious paintings, celebrating Tutankhamun's arrival in the afterlife.

A large statue of a jackal guarded the entrance from the burial chamber into the treasury, where more marvels were placed, including another shrine surrounded by the statues of four goddesses. Within this shrine was a chest made of alabaster containing four miniature coffins, made of gold, to hold the embalmed organs of the king.

Tutankhamun died without an heir, and his death left his widow, Ankhesenamun, powerless and alone. We know

WINGED SCARAB
This pendant from the king's tomb is made of gold and semiprecious stones. The design spells the three hieroglyphs of Tutankhamun's name.

GOLDEN MASK
The king's famous death mask was wrought from thick gold plate. It weighs 22½ lb (10.2 kg). The broad breast plate, inlaid with glass, has a banded collar with falcon-headed clasps.

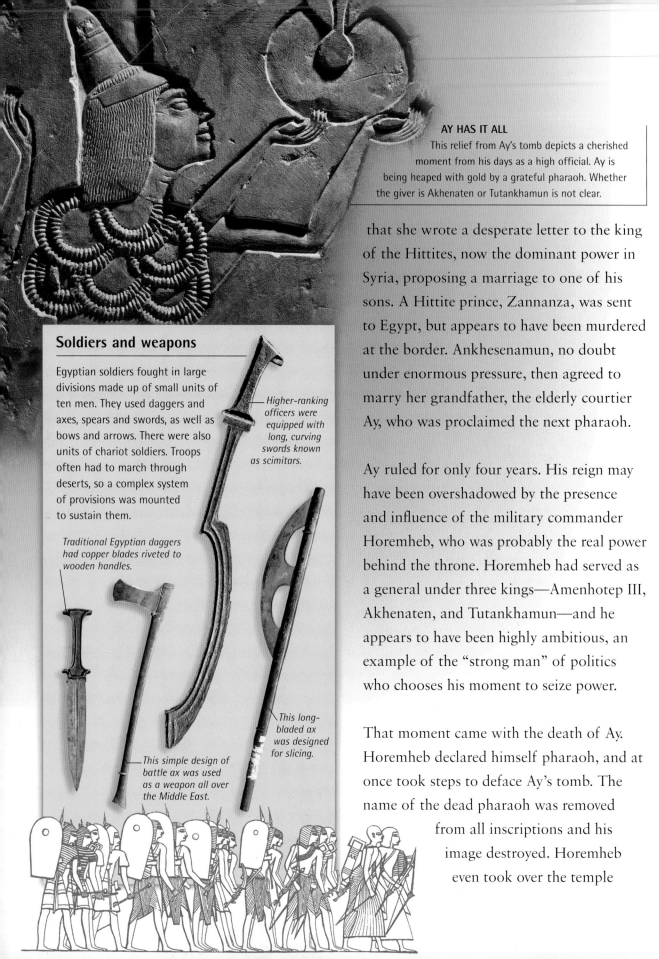

AY HAS IT ALL

This relief from Ay's tomb depicts a cherished moment from his days as a high official. Ay is being heaped with gold by a grateful pharaoh. Whether the giver is Akhenaten or Tutankhamun is not clear.

Soldiers and weapons

Egyptian soldiers fought in large divisions made up of small units of ten men. They used daggers and axes, spears and swords, as well as bows and arrows. There were also units of chariot soldiers. Troops often had to march through deserts, so a complex system of provisions was mounted to sustain them.

Traditional Egyptian daggers had copper blades riveted to wooden handles.

Higher-ranking officers were equipped with long, curving swords known as scimitars.

This long-bladed ax was designed for slicing.

This simple design of battle ax was used as a weapon all over the Middle East.

that she wrote a desperate letter to the king of the Hittites, now the dominant power in Syria, proposing a marriage to one of his sons. A Hittite prince, Zannanza, was sent to Egypt, but appears to have been murdered at the border. Ankhesenamun, no doubt under enormous pressure, then agreed to marry her grandfather, the elderly courtier Ay, who was proclaimed the next pharaoh.

Ay ruled for only four years. His reign may have been overshadowed by the presence and influence of the military commander Horemheb, who was probably the real power behind the throne. Horemheb had served as a general under three kings—Amenhotep III, Akhenaten, and Tutankhamun—and he appears to have been highly ambitious, an example of the "strong man" of politics who chooses his moment to seize power.

That moment came with the death of Ay. Horemheb declared himself pharaoh, and at once took steps to deface Ay's tomb. The name of the dead pharaoh was removed from all inscriptions and his image destroyed. Horemheb even took over the temple

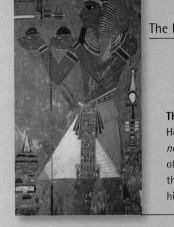

THE GENERAL KING
Horemheb, wearing the *nemes* headdress, makes offerings to various gods in this fine wall painting from his Valley of the Kings tomb.

dedicated to his predecessor. He seems to have been determined to remove Ay's name from history, and to pretend that he had never existed.

Horemheb did not come from royal blood, although he married a sister of Nefertiti in order to forge a connection with the royal family. He needed to bolster his claim to rule as pharaoh, therefore, and he sought to link himself directly with Amenhotep III, the most powerful and prosperous pharaoh of the 18th Dynasty. So he set about removing the names and identities of all four pharaohs standing between himself and Amenhotep III—not only Ay, but also Tutankhamun, Smenkhkare, and Akhenaten. In the same spirit, he demolished Amarna, the city built by Akhenaten in honor of the Aten. The site was abandoned, and the ruins of its once-magnificent buildings were covered by the drifting sands. All memory of the place disappeared from history until it was discovered by chance 3,000 years later.

CAPTIVES OF HOREMHEB
A scene from Horemheb's second tomb at Saqqara records a military victory. Guards are leading captive women and children by the arm. The hands of male prisoners are fastened with wooden cuffs.

Horemheb reigned for some 30 years, during which time he strengthened his iron grip on the country. He rebuilt many temples, and appointed former soldiers as priests, so tightening his hold on the state religion. Horemheb also began a war against the Hittites in northern Syria, a war that would continue under subsequent pharaohs. He chose his military deputy, Paramessu, as his heir. This commander ascended the throne as Ramesses I, and was the founder of the mighty 19th Dynasty, the dynasty that presided over the last great flowering of Egyptian civilization.

CHAPTER EIGHT

The *Ramesside* kings

Under the 19th Dynasty, Egypt became great once more. The dynasty's first pharaoh, Ramesses I, was in his fifties when he succeeded to the throne, and he reigned for only two years. He was the first of the rulers known as the Ramesside kings.

I T WAS HIS SON, SETI I, who established the true character of the dynasty. Seti made it his mission to restore Egypt's glory. On a great list of Egyptian kings inscribed for him, no mention is made of any of the pharaohs between Amenhotep III and Horemheb. It was as if the kings connected to Akhenaten had never reigned.

Seti made up for their years of weak foreign policy by being an energetic military commander. He led a number of campaigns in Palestine and Syria, and seems to have won back some cities lost to the kingdom of the Hittites in northern Syria during Akhenaten's reign. He also repelled raids by Libyan tribesmen who attacked Egypt from the Western Desert. To Nubia in the south he sent expeditions to secure gold to pay for his wars; he also found there a supply of slaves to work on his vast building programs.

◀ Colossal head of Ramesses II at Luxor Temple

HALL OF DARKNESS
Seti I's Great Hypostyle Hall has 134 gigantic columns that supported a stone roof. "Hypostyle" is a Greek word meaning "resting on pillars." Small slits high in the walls admitted the only light.

THE TOMB OF OSIRIS
The ruins of Seti's Osireion, the tomb of Osiris, can still be seen. An underground hall was surrounded by a canal of spring water, representing the island that arose from chaos at the moment of creation.

Seti was a great repairer and builder of monuments. He began the famous "Hypostyle" Hall at Karnak, the largest pillared hall of this kind ever built and a true wonder of ancient architecture. At Abydos, Seti erected a large temple to Osiris and behind it built a mysterious underground structure known as the "Osireion," which was popularly believed to hold the tomb of Osiris himself. In the Valley of the Kings, Seti built the deepest of all burial chambers, at the end of a long descending corridor some 300 ft (90 m) within the rock, where his alabaster sarcophagus lay surrounded by wall paintings of the underworld.

Seti's son, Ramesses II, is generally held by historians to have been the most powerful pharaoh in Egyptian history. He reigned for 67 years and is known as "Ramesses the Great." He

A NEW BEGINNING
Seti sports a fine wig in this exquisite relief. His 13-year reign began a period of renewal for Egypt. Its empire was strengthened, and art and culture reached a new level of sophistication.

believed that greatness was his birthright. From a young age he was trained in the arts of war and conquest, and early in his reign he gathered a great army to attack the Hittites outside the city of Kadesh in Syria. The battle was a key event in Ramesses's long reign and was celebrated in stone throughout Egypt as a great personal victory.

In fact, the battle of Kadesh was not a very glorious encounter. Spies deceived the Egyptians into thinking that the main Hittite army was far from Kadesh, and Ramesses marched his division straight into an ambush. Hittite chariots scattered the Egyptian soldiers like chaff, and defeat seemed inevitable had it not been for the pharaoh's personal bravery in rallying his remaining troops in the thick of battle. Eventually, the day ended in a stalemate with both sides exhausted from fighting. When it became clear that there was no glory or victory to be gained from such a war, the Hittites and the Egyptians signed a peace treaty—the first in history. But the peace marked the decline of Egyptian influence in Syria and Palestine.

KING OF KINGS
This black granite statue of Ramesses II, looking the supreme victor in his Blue Crown (the war crown), is probably the finest of the hundreds of surviving statues of the pharaoh.

The Hittite king donated a young daughter to Ramesses as a way of maintaining the peace between the two powers. She joined a harem of royal wives that over the years produced more than a hundred sons and untold numbers of daughters for the pharaoh. In previous years, the harem had been dominated by his Great Royal Wife, Nefertari. She is one of the most famous queens in Egyptian history and her image was worshiped all over the country. She died in about year 23 of Ramesses's reign, and the decorations within her burial chamber in the Valley of the Queens are of unmatched excellence.

HAREM POPULATION
The royal harem was home not only to the king's favorite wives and foreign brides, but also to women who were widowed, unattached, or ambitious.

GREAT ROYAL WIFE
Nefertari, seen here in a splendid feathered crown with vulture headdress, makes offerings to the gods in this painting from her lavish tomb.

Nefertari's status is evidence that women could often play a powerful role in ancient Egypt. It was a society that gave women more legal protection than any of the other ancient societies. A woman could enter into contracts and had property rights. She could even sue her husband for adultery or mistreatment.

The pharaoh's Great Royal Wife could sometimes wield an enormous influence in the Egyptian court and over Egyptian religion. The queen had married a living god, and so became a deity herself. She was "God's Wife of Amun" and took her

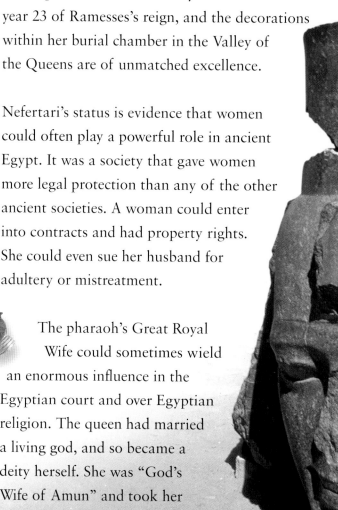

place beside the pharaoh in various religious rituals. If the pharaoh was still a boy when he came to the throne, then his mother would often rule the country in his place.

The power of the pharaohs was expressed through monumental buildings, and Ramesses II built on a scale unprecedented since the Pyramid Age. He constructed and enlarged temples all over Egypt, and outside them he set up colossal statues of himself. These portray him with a serene smile and a distant gaze, as if surveying the mightiness of his works. Three thousand workers were employed to build his vast mortuary temple, the Ramesseum, on the west bank of the Nile near Thebes. In its outer courtyard, there stood a statue of the pharaoh that rose to a height of 60 ft (18 m). It was carved from black granite and weighed more than 1,000 tons.

The name of Ramesses II appears on hundreds of monuments throughout the country. The smallest repair or rebuilding of a previous pharaoh's monument gave Ramesses the excuse to have his name carved all over it, so determined was he to immortalize his name.

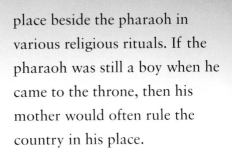

RAMESSES THE COLOSSUS
This colossal pink granite statue of Ramesses II towers before the entrance to the Great Hypostyle Hall at Karnak. The tiny figure standing at his feet may represent Nefertari, or else a daughter who became his wife.

FALLEN POWER
A shattered head of Ramesses II lies in pieces in a courtyard of the Ramesseum. Few images are more evocative of Egypt's fallen greatness.

However, the greatest symbol of Ramesses's power, even greater than the Ramesseum, was created at Abu Simbel in Nubia. Here the Great Temple of Ramesses, and a smaller temple dedicated to the goddess Hathor and Queen Nefertari, were carved out of a cliff face above the Nile. In front of the Great Temple are four gigantic figures of the seated pharaoh. The temple itself extends 200 ft (60 m) into the cliff.

The builders excavated the temple with such accuracy that at the equinoxes in February and October, when day and night are of equal length, the rays of the rising sun flood directly through the entrance and bathe in light three great statues of the gods. The Great Temple is an extraordinary accomplishment that can be compared with anything created by the pharaohs of the Old Kingdom. And then—if that were not achievement enough—Ramesses built a marvelous new city, known as Per-Ramesse ("the Domain of Ramesses"), in the northeastern Delta. It was filled with great avenues, obelisks, and monuments of his reign, but most traces of the city disappeared long ago.

Ramesses II died at the age of 92, if the chronological record is accurate, but he was already a god. Statues of him entitled "Ramesses the God" were worshiped in temples throughout the land. His tomb has long since been ransacked, its treasures scattered to the winds. But his mummy survives—part of the hoard discovered at Deir el-Bahri in the 19th century.

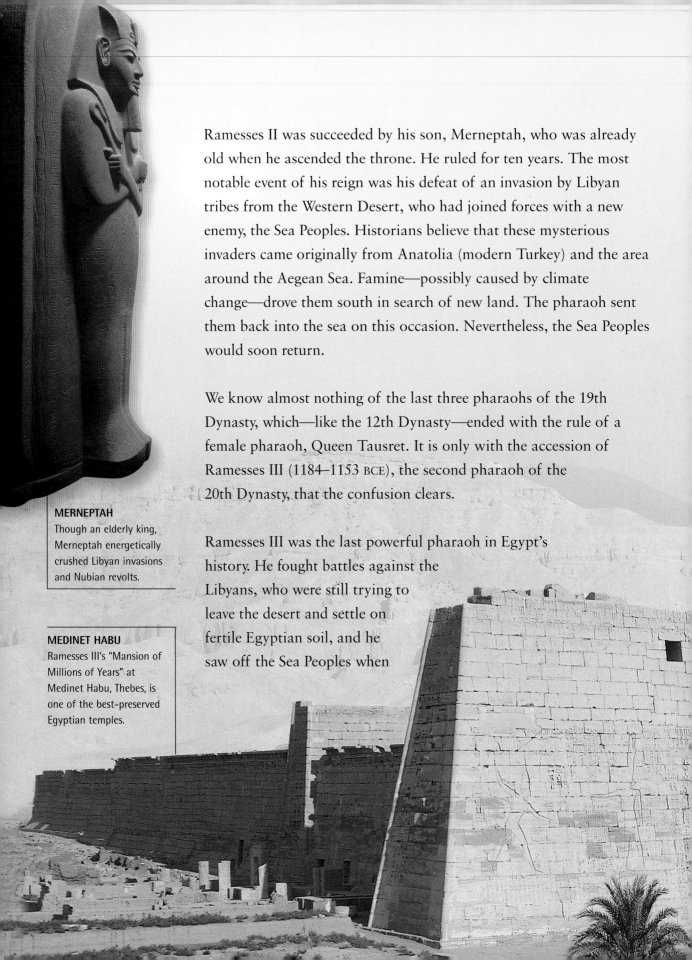

Ramesses II was succeeded by his son, Merneptah, who was already old when he ascended the throne. He ruled for ten years. The most notable event of his reign was his defeat of an invasion by Libyan tribes from the Western Desert, who had joined forces with a new enemy, the Sea Peoples. Historians believe that these mysterious invaders came originally from Anatolia (modern Turkey) and the area around the Aegean Sea. Famine—possibly caused by climate change—drove them south in search of new land. The pharaoh sent them back into the sea on this occasion. Nevertheless, the Sea Peoples would soon return.

We know almost nothing of the last three pharaohs of the 19th Dynasty, which—like the 12th Dynasty—ended with the rule of a female pharaoh, Queen Tausret. It is only with the accession of Ramesses III (1184–1153 BCE), the second pharaoh of the 20th Dynasty, that the confusion clears.

Ramesses III was the last powerful pharaoh in Egypt's history. He fought battles against the Libyans, who were still trying to leave the desert and settle on fertile Egyptian soil, and he saw off the Sea Peoples when

MERNEPTAH
Though an elderly king, Merneptah energetically crushed Libyan invasions and Nubian revolts.

MEDINET HABU
Ramesses III's "Mansion of Millions of Years" at Medinet Habu, Thebes, is one of the best-preserved Egyptian temples.

MENACE FROM THE SEA
Ramesses III's victory over the Sea Peoples is recorded in this carved relief at Medinet Habu. The artist has taken care to show the Sea Peoples' strange horned helmets, tunics, and shields.

they again attacked Egypt from the sea. The Egyptians were not skilled sailors, and were unused to fighting sea battles. But the Sea Peoples sailed their ships into one of the waterways of the Delta. Ramesses positioned his archers on the shore and in moored boats. As the Sea People's ships drew near, the Egyptian bowmen, expert in their art, launched great showers of arrows against them and destroyed them.

But if he conquered his external enemies, Ramesses was not so successful with his opponents in Egypt itself. During his reign, the priests of the major temples began to acquire enormous wealth and power. Ramesses III himself gave great estates

DRESSED TO IMPRESS
Decked out in full court dress, complete with a gold-fringed White Crown and a magnificent kilt, Ramesses III makes offerings to the gods in this fine relief.

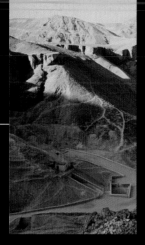

VALLEY OF THE THIEVES
Valley of the Kings tombs were not concealed. They were simply protected by a closed stone door and a seal. This made them easy for the robbers to target.

TOMB RAIDERS
Tomb robbers were often the very same people who had dug the tombs, and who knew its traps and obstacles. The mummy itself was a prize, since its bandages contained many small, portable treasures.

of land to the priestly caste, and as a result, less grain flowed into the royal granaries than before. There was famine and poverty. Grain shortages led to the first recorded official workers' strike in the world's history.

During these troubled times, a plot was hatched to assassinate the king as he took part in a religious festival. The plans were discovered, and the conspirators were put on trial. Among the plotters were certain wives of the pharaoh, who were later accused of "stirring up the people… in order to make rebellion against their lord." It is an

indication of Egypt's unhappy state that they believed they might succeed in this purpose.

Ramesses III died soon after the plot was discovered. He was followed by a series of short-lived pharaohs who all took the name of Ramesses until the very end of the 20th Dynasty. Their reigns are not recorded in any detail, except for accounts of expeditions into the desert in search of gold and stone. It seems to have been in this period that kingship finally lost its divine aura. The pharaoh was no longer a living god. Instead, he was simply the gods' representative on earth.

Egypt was in decline. Its frontiers shrank, and there were frequent invasions of Libyans. The Egyptians no longer controlled Palestine and large areas of Syria. There were periodic famines and workers' strikes. And, perhaps most significantly, the tombs of the ancient pharaohs were robbed and systematically stripped of their gold.

The increase in tomb robbery suggests a deep crisis in Egyptian society and in its system of belief. The cult of the dead no longer protected their burial places. We know from court records that a ring of thieves was put on trial for robbing tombs in the reign of

OFFICIAL BREAK-IN
This restoration of Ramesses VI's shattered sarcophagus lid was completed in 2004. Some have suggested that the huge granite coffin could not have been broken by tomb robbers and must have been opened on the orders of government officials in need of gold.

THE KING UNTHRONED
In this imagined scene, the unlucky Ramesses XI is being stripped of his sovereignty over Upper Egypt by Herihor, the powerful high priest of Amun.

Ramesses IX, but the theft of grave goods continued for many more centuries. There came a time, in fact, when scarcely one of the great tombs remained unscathed. It even appears that officials at the high temple of Thebes itself engaged in tomb-robbing, either to enrich themselves with gold or to bolster Egypt's failing economy.

THE POWER OF AMUN
A fine red-granite head is all that remains of this cult statue of Amun. The god's prestige was the source of the Theban priests' power.

One unhappy tale serves to illustrate just how low Egypt's prestige had fallen by the end of the New Kingdom. During the reign of Ramesses XI (1099–1069 BCE), the last pharaoh of the 20th Dynasty, a temple official from Thebes named Wenamun was sent to the Phoenician port of Byblos (in modern-day Lebanon). His mission was to obtain precious cedar wood to repair the leaks in the sacred barque of Amun. In the days of Egypt's glory, a priest of Amun would have been treated with great respect by his foreign hosts. Instead, Wenamun was forced to take passage in a foreign ship, and because he was robbed along the way, he was held prisoner in Byblos until new funds were sent from Egypt. Even then he was charged an exorbitant price for the wood.

At home, the pharaoh's authority was weakened by the growing power of the Theban priesthood. Their vast estates of land meant that they now controlled most of Egypt's wealth. They also owned 90 percent of all ships, and 80 percent of factories and workshops. Hundreds of government offices were in their hands.

Eventually, toward the end of the 20th Dynasty, a powerful high priest of Amun named Herihor, who was also an army general, made himself priest-king in the south of Egypt, while recognizing the rule of Ramesses XI in the north. Egypt had again split into two halves. In temple reliefs at Karnak, Herihor is depicted on the same scale as the king, and his name is written inside a royal cartouche.

SUPREME PRIEST
Herihor also held the title of vizier (prime minister) when he staged his *coup d'état*. Although a priest, he had an army background.

When Ramesses XI died, the throne passed to a pharaoh known as Smendes (1069–1043 BCE), the founder of the 21st Dynasty. This pharaoh moved his capital to Tanis, in the Delta. Once again, there were two main centers of power in Egypt—that of the high priests at Thebes in the south, and that of the pharaoh in the north. But the confusion went further than this. Egypt was fragmenting into a number of independent provinces and local kingdoms as certain families grew rich and powerful by taking control of various state and religious offices.

This was the beginning of the Third Intermediate Period (1069–715 BCE). After 2,000 years, the glorious achievements of the Egyptian pharaohs were coming to an end. Although Egyptian civilization would continue for another 1,000 years, the story from now on is one of steady decline.

CHAPTER NINE

Twilight *of the* gods

By 1000 BCE, Egypt was no longer the center of the civilized world. Instead, it found itself on the fringe of the wider Mediterranean community where other, newer powers saw in Egypt's growing weakness a target for their own ambition and greed.

IN THE LAST MILLENNIUM of its history, ancient Egypt would be ruled by dynasties of foreign pharaohs and by a series of outside invaders. However, there would be peaks as well as troughs in this process of decline— times when Egypt again became a military presence in the Middle East, times when native Egyptians were able to resist their foreign rulers and take back power for themselves. And we should not necessarily assume that for ordinary Egyptians, life was always hard or miserable. The world changes, but lives go on. People survive, and even welcome, change.

Very little is recorded about the deeds of the kings of the 21st Dynasty. We know that Egyptian control over Nubia was lost after many centuries of domination. The enormous wealth of the earlier kingdoms was gone, and the building of grand royal monuments came to an end.

◀ Reconstruction of the Temple of Isis at Philae (Ptolemaic period)

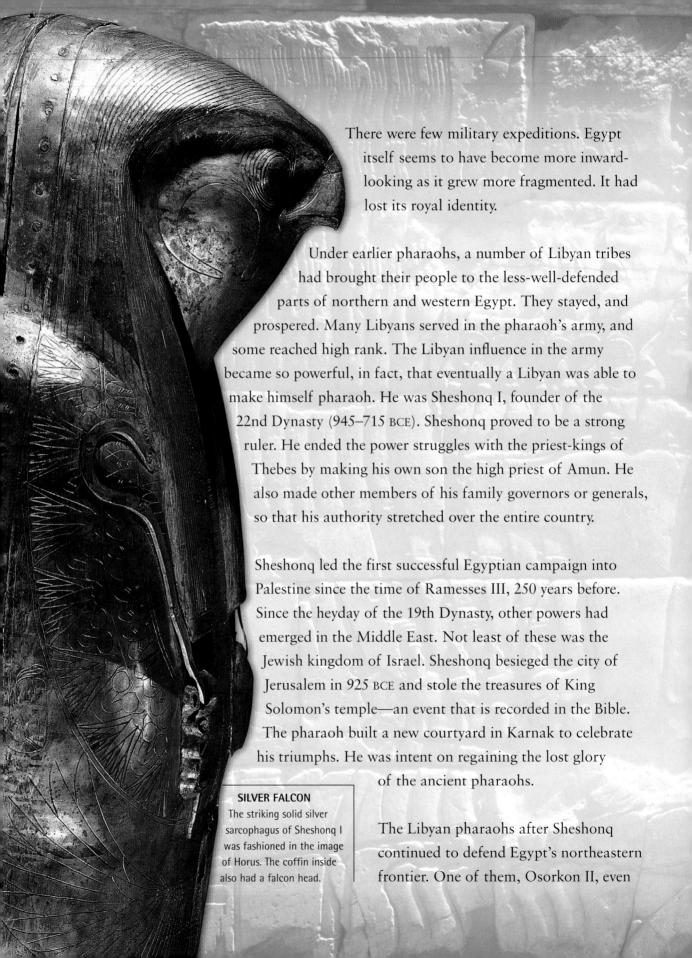

There were few military expeditions. Egypt itself seems to have become more inward-looking as it grew more fragmented. It had lost its royal identity.

Under earlier pharaohs, a number of Libyan tribes had brought their people to the less-well-defended parts of northern and western Egypt. They stayed, and prospered. Many Libyans served in the pharaoh's army, and some reached high rank. The Libyan influence in the army became so powerful, in fact, that eventually a Libyan was able to make himself pharaoh. He was Sheshonq I, founder of the 22nd Dynasty (945–715 BCE). Sheshonq proved to be a strong ruler. He ended the power struggles with the priest-kings of Thebes by making his own son the high priest of Amun. He also made other members of his family governors or generals, so that his authority stretched over the entire country.

Sheshonq led the first successful Egyptian campaign into Palestine since the time of Ramesses III, 250 years before. Since the heyday of the 19th Dynasty, other powers had emerged in the Middle East. Not least of these was the Jewish kingdom of Israel. Sheshonq besieged the city of Jerusalem in 925 BCE and stole the treasures of King Solomon's temple—an event that is recorded in the Bible. The pharaoh built a new courtyard in Karnak to celebrate his triumphs. He was intent on regaining the lost glory of the ancient pharaohs.

SILVER FALCON
The striking solid silver sarcophagus of Sheshonq I was fashioned in the image of Horus. The coffin inside also had a falcon head.

The Libyan pharaohs after Sheshonq continued to defend Egypt's northeastern frontier. One of them, Osorkon II, even

formed an alliance
with the Israelites in
order to stop the
advance of a new
menace in the Middle
East, the Assyrian empire. But Sheshonq's successors
could not hold on to power in all of Egypt, and the
old division with the priests of Thebes reemerged.
The history of the times is confused, but the kings of
the 22nd Dynasty seem to have shared power with
two breakaway dynasties—the 23rd and the 24th.

In this chaotic situation, the rule of Egypt was
snatched by an invader. In 730 BCE, Piy, the king of
Nubia, advanced northward along the Nile and
conquered the major cities in his path. In previous
centuries, the land of Nubia had
been a province and trading
post of Egypt. Nubia's rich
resources—particularly
of gold, ivory, and
slaves—were exploited
by the pharaohs for
their own purposes. But
since the days of the 19th
Dynasty, Nubia had been
an independent power. The kings

TOMBS OF TANIS
The 21st Dynasty kings were buried at
Tanis, in the Delta. Some were found
inside reused New Kingdom royal coffins,
which suggests that the Valley of the
Kings was by now being officially looted.

THE GOLDEN THREE
This beautiful gold trinity
of Horus, Osiris, and Isis
was made for Osorkon II.
It was probably stolen from
the king's tomb at Tanis.

MASK OF SHESHONQ II
This gold funeral mask belonging to Sheshonq II
is among the finest found at Tanis. Even so, the
quality of its craftsmanship is poor compared
with the mask of Tutankhamun.

MAGIC CHARM

This amulet was found at the great rock of Gebel Barkal, the cult center of Amun in Nubia. It incorporates several magical symbols, including the ankh, the so-called *djed* pillar (the "backbone of Osiris"), and a dog-headed scepter. The god Heh at the top represents everlasting life.

of Nubia had their capital at Napata, between the third and fourth cataracts of the Nile. Now they were strong enough to defeat their ancient overlords and to conquer Egypt itself. It is a measure of how far Egypt had fallen from its old might.

And so it happened that Piy became the first pharaoh of the 25th Dynasty (747–656 BCE) and began a period of Nubian rule over Egypt that lasted for almost a hundred years. Since the time of the New Kingdom, the Nubians had worshiped Amun as

PYRAMIDS OF MEROE

There are the remains of more than a hundred pyramids in Nubia. The first were built at Napata in about 700 BCE when the Nubian kings ruled Egypt. In about 300 BCE, the capital moved to Meroe and a great pyramid field was built there (*above*).

their chief god. Piy and his successors went to great pains to restore Amun's prestige throughout Egypt and to identify themselves with the pharaohs of Egypt's glorious past.

The Nubian pharaohs used the ancient religious center of Memphis as their capital, and publicly worshiped the old gods. They wore the crowns and regalia of the Egyptian pharaohs and were buried in the same manner, having their bodies embalmed and mummified. The Nubians even began to build pyramids once more, though their royal pyramids were smaller and steeper than those of the Old Kingdom rulers. Even the art associated with the Old Kingdom was revived. It was a way of reclaiming Egypt's identity by reconnecting with its past. But this return to normality was soon threatened.

By 700 BCE, the Assyrian empire was the supreme power in the Middle East, and was greatly feared. Its territories stretched from the Persian Gulf in the east as far as Palestine in the west, from where it was poised to harass Egypt itself. When the Palestinians rose up against their hated overlords, the Nubian pharaoh Shebitku sent an army to help the

NUBIAN PRIEST
As in Thebes, the priesthood of Amun grew so powerful in Nubia that there, too, it was able to usurp the local kings and form a dynasty.

rebels. It was defeated, but the Egyptians continued to mount further campaigns against the Assyrians in Palestine.

Eventually, the Assyrians attacked Egypt. Their first invasion was beaten back, but they tried again in 671 BCE, and this time they captured Memphis, driving the pharaoh from the city. In 664 BCE, an Assyrian army ransacked Thebes and destroyed the sacred treasures of the temple of Amun. The Nubian pharaohs fled back to Napata.

GREAT TAHARQO
This shabti figure is of Taharqo, perhaps the greatest of the Nubian pharaohs. His huge pyramid near Napata may have been inspired by the Giza pyramids, which he could see from his palace at Memphis.

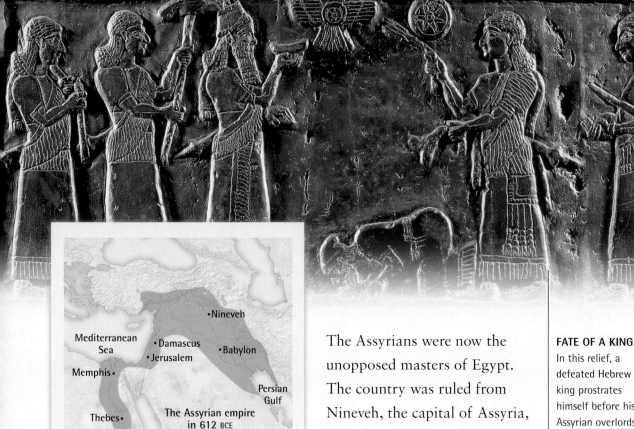

The Assyrian empire

The Assyrians were the first people to unite the Near East into one empire. They originally lived in the hills around the Tigris River in what is now northern Iraq. In the 9th century BCE, they began to conquer the surrounding kingdoms in the name of their chief god, Ashur. Assyrian armies ruthlessly destroyed the cities in their path, including Thebes, and deported defeated people as slaves to distant parts of the empire. A well-organized system of imperial government extracted heavy tributes from the conquered lands. By 612 BCE, the empire was too large to control and was defeated by an army of Babylonians and Medes (warriors from Persia).

PSAMTEK

Psamtek I's mummy has survived. Although he threw the Assyrians out of Egypt, Psamtek did not want their empire to collapse. A power vacuum would have been unsafe for Egypt.

The Assyrians were now the unopposed masters of Egypt. The country was ruled from Nineveh, the capital of Assyria, and a local Egyptian king named Psamtek was appointed to govern Egypt in its name. Thus began the era known to historians as the Late Period. It was truly the twilight of ancient Egyptian history, and would witness the last Egyptian to rule over his country for 2,500 years.

Psamtek proved a disobedient servant to his Assyrian overlords and organized a successful rebellion against them. He extended his control over the rest of the country and, as Psamtek I, began the 26th Dynasty of pharaonic power. He had previously been king of a region known as Sais in the Delta, and his dynasty become known as the Saite Dynasty. There was a brief revival of Egyptian power under the Saite pharaohs. Psamtek built a series of fortresses and garrison towns in the Delta to defend the newly liberated Egypt, and

FATE OF A KING

In this relief, a defeated Hebrew king prostrates himself before his Assyrian overlords. Egypt was next to share Israel's fate.

even fought in the east. His successors continued his campaigns, and when the Assyrian empire fell in 612 BCE, the Egyptians were able to invade and occupy Palestine once again.

Trade flourished under the Saite pharaohs and Egypt again became prosperous. They built extensively, enlarging and restoring cult sites at Memphis, Karnak, and elsewhere. The art of the period can be compared favorably with that of any other era of Egyptian history. It is as if the native strengths of the country were reasserting themselves before finally being vanquished for good.

Another group of foreign conquerors, this time the Persians, now invaded Egypt. In little more than 20 years, the Persians had created the largest empire the world had yet seen, stretching from the shores of the Black Sea to the Red Sea and across the Iranian plateau as far as Afghanistan and the Indus River. In 525 BCE, the Persian king Cambyses added Egypt to his list of conquests.

The Persians ruled Egypt for the next 150 years through provincial governors called satraps. The Persian kings took care to respect Egyptian customs. They adopted Egyptian royal titles (they are the 27th Dynasty in Egyptian history) and worshiped Egyptian gods. But there is no doubt that most Egyptians hated their rule. There were various uprisings, savagely put down by the Persians, but in the early 5th century BCE the Egyptians managed to regain their independence under a prince of Sais named Amyrtaeus. He founded the 28th Dynasty (404–399 BCE), and was its sole king.

After Amyrtaeus there followed two more dynasties of native pharaohs. The 29th and 30th Dynasties lasted

THE PERSIAN IMMORTALS
This glazed-brick frieze from the palace of the Persian king Darius shows one of his elite corps known as "the Immortals." There were always 10,000 of them. If one died, he was instantly replaced, so that the corps seemed to defy death.

HEAD OF NECTANEBO

Nectanebo I, founder of the 30th Dynasty, successfully pushed a combined force of Greeks and Persians out of Egypt. During his stable, 18-year rule, he restored many of Egypt's dilapidated temples.

just over 60 years (380–343 BCE) and included five pharaohs. We know them from the tombs and temples they built. Once more, Egyptian pharaohs were carrying on the work of their ancestors, thus ensuring the astonishing continuities of Egyptian history. This is a very murky period of history, however. There were plots and counter-plots, family rivalries and blood feuds. The

PRESENTS FOR PERSIA

In this relief, subjects are taking gifts to Persia. Each year, emissaries from Egypt would travel to the Persian capital, Persepolis, with tributes.

ALEXANDER THE GREAT

Alexander is seen here with his legendary steed, Bucephalus. His personal motive for fighting the Persians was to win everlasting fame and glory.

pharaohs hired mercenaries to fight in their armies and played a dangerous game of foreign politics, acting with Persia's enemies to keep the Persian empire at bay. But they lost the game. In 343 BCE, the pharaoh Nectanebo II, at the head of a large army including some 20,000 Greek mercenary soldiers, met a Persian force led by

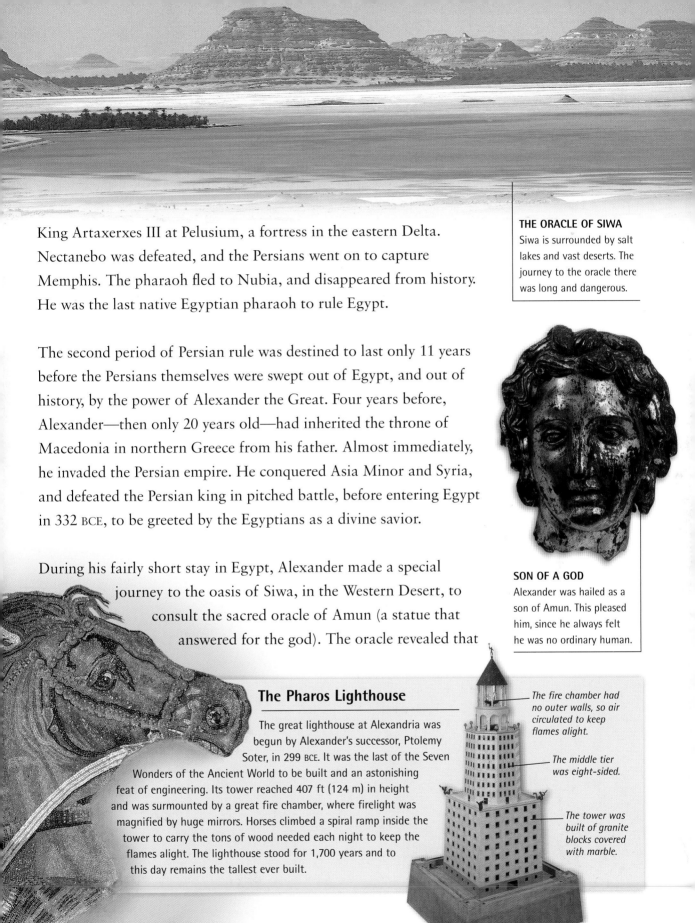

King Artaxerxes III at Pelusium, a fortress in the eastern Delta. Nectanebo was defeated, and the Persians went on to capture Memphis. The pharaoh fled to Nubia, and disappeared from history. He was the last native Egyptian pharaoh to rule Egypt.

The second period of Persian rule was destined to last only 11 years before the Persians themselves were swept out of Egypt, and out of history, by the power of Alexander the Great. Four years before, Alexander—then only 20 years old—had inherited the throne of Macedonia in northern Greece from his father. Almost immediately, he invaded the Persian empire. He conquered Asia Minor and Syria, and defeated the Persian king in pitched battle, before entering Egypt in 332 BCE, to be greeted by the Egyptians as a divine savior.

During his fairly short stay in Egypt, Alexander made a special journey to the oasis of Siwa, in the Western Desert, to consult the sacred oracle of Amun (a statue that answered for the god). The oracle revealed that

THE ORACLE OF SIWA
Siwa is surrounded by salt lakes and vast deserts. The journey to the oracle there was long and dangerous.

SON OF A GOD
Alexander was hailed as a son of Amun. This pleased him, since he always felt he was no ordinary human.

The Pharos Lighthouse

The great lighthouse at Alexandria was begun by Alexander's successor, Ptolemy Soter, in 299 BCE. It was the last of the Seven Wonders of the Ancient World to be built and an astonishing feat of engineering. Its tower reached 407 ft (124 m) in height and was surmounted by a great fire chamber, where firelight was magnified by huge mirrors. Horses climbed a spiral ramp inside the tower to carry the tons of wood needed each night to keep the flames alight. The lighthouse stood for 1,700 years and to this day remains the tallest ever built.

The fire chamber had no outer walls, so air circulated to keep flames alight.

The middle tier was eight-sided.

The tower was built of granite blocks covered with marble.

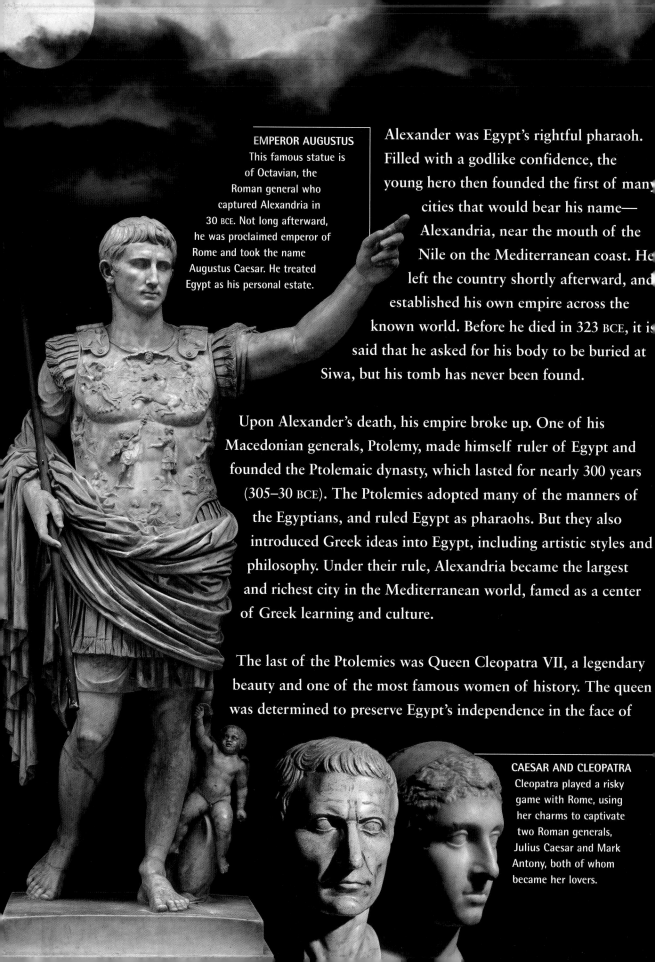

Alexander was Egypt's rightful pharaoh. Filled with a godlike confidence, the young hero then founded the first of many cities that would bear his name— Alexandria, near the mouth of the Nile on the Mediterranean coast. He left the country shortly afterward, and established his own empire across the known world. Before he died in 323 BCE, it is said that he asked for his body to be buried at Siwa, but his tomb has never been found.

Upon Alexander's death, his empire broke up. One of his Macedonian generals, Ptolemy, made himself ruler of Egypt and founded the Ptolemaic dynasty, which lasted for nearly 300 years (305–30 BCE). The Ptolemies adopted many of the manners of the Egyptians, and ruled Egypt as pharaohs. But they also introduced Greek ideas into Egypt, including artistic styles and philosophy. Under their rule, Alexandria became the largest and richest city in the Mediterranean world, famed as a center of Greek learning and culture.

The last of the Ptolemies was Queen Cleopatra VII, a legendary beauty and one of the most famous women of history. The queen was determined to preserve Egypt's independence in the face of

CAESAR AND CLEOPATRA
Cleopatra played a risky game with Rome, using her charms to captivate two Roman generals, Julius Caesar and Mark Antony, both of whom became her lovers.

the Mediterranean's latest menace, Rome. This new power was fast transforming from a republic into an empire, and had its eyes on Egypt. But Cleopatra's efforts to keep Rome at bay were in vain. As Roman forces entered Alexandria in 30 BCE, the queen killed herself rather than be taken as a trophy in a Roman triumph.

Following Cleopatra's death, Egypt became the treasure house and granary of the Roman empire. The fertile Nile Valley fed the empire's growing population, with tons of Egyptian grain shipped all over the Mediterranean each year. The Romans founded many new cities in Egypt, which once again became a rich and prosperous region. Although the Roman emperors continued to build some temples in the Egyptian style, the new cities were of the classical Roman design, with a forum, paved streets, public baths, and amphitheaters.

Roman soldiers wandered among the remnants of Egypt's glory, already ancient, and marveled. These were temples and monuments and pyramids built thousands of years before their arrival. What kind of civilization had been here? Its culture and technology rivaled anything produced by Rome. What great rulers had erected such massive memorials to the dead? What people had lived in such close communion with the afterlife? Small wonder that the ancient Egyptians still have the power to haunt the human imagination after thousands of years.

LASTING GLORY
The wreck of a colossal statue of Ramesses II lies in a courtyard of his temple. Though its temples are now ruined, it is easy for us to see how great Egypt and its kings once were.

Reference
section

◀ Death mask of Tutankhamun c. 1324 BCE

Clues to the past

OUR KNOWLEDGE OF ANCIENT EGYPT comes from a variety of sources, ancient and modern. We have the eyewitness accounts of ancient historians; archaeologists excavate historical sites to find mummies, tombs, and artifacts; scholars decipher hieroglyphs, the writing of ancient Egypt; and scientists use dating and imaging technology to examine ancient objects, including mummies.

Eyewitness accounts

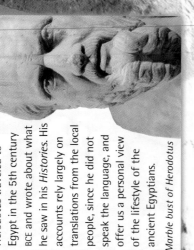

The Greek historian Herodotus traveled to Egypt in the 5th century BCE and wrote about what he saw in his *Histories*. His accounts rely largely on translations from the local people, since he did not speak the language, and offer us a personal view of the lifestyle of the ancient Egyptians.

Marble bust of Herodotus

Hieroglyphs

The first hieroglyphs were simple.

Hieroglyphs are very useful for piecing together Egypt's history. Much information about religious beliefs, the reigns of kings, court cases, trade, and politics has come from reading hieroglyphs. They were first used in the 4th millennium BCE to record the names of kings and officials. Scholars have been able to read hieroglyphs since 1832 and can often tell when they were written from their style and complexity.

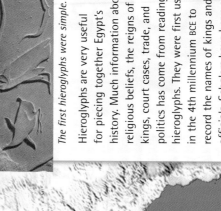

An archaeologist opens an undisturbed tomb.

Archaeology

Archaeologists are people who excavate historical sites in search of clues to the past. Not all their work is in search of treasure and tombs. Analysing the garbage that ancient people threw away can tell us much about daily life. Studying ancient foundations can reveal how long-vanished cities were laid out.

Rosetta

Alexandria

Heliopolis

Cairo

Giza
Abusir
Saqqara
Memphis

Meidum

Hawara
Ahnas
(Heracleopolis)

LOWER EGYPT

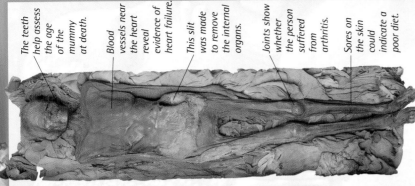

The teeth help assess the age of the mummy at death.

Blood vessels near the heart reveal evidence of heart failure.

This slit was made to remove the internal organs.

Joints show whether the person suffered from arthritis.

Sores on the skin could indicate a poor diet.

Mummy of woman c. 600 BCE

Mummies

The Egyptians went to great lengths to mummify their dead. Mummies are time capsules that give us much information about the diet, diseases, and environment of people living thousands of years ago. For example, the teeth of the woman shown above have been worn from a lifetime of chewing gritty bread. Scientists can even identify the plant oils used to preserve her skin.

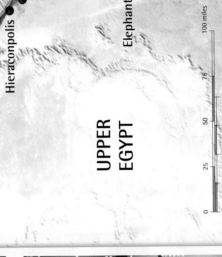

UPPER EGYPT

Abydos • Dendera • Luxor (Thebes) • Hieraconpolis • Edfu • Aswan • Elephantine • Philae • Abu Simbel •

This CAT scan uses a rotating ring to reflect X-rays onto a mummy.

Technology

Today, we can find out about mummies without unwrapping the bandages or opening the body and causing damage. X-rays, which give pictures of hard objects, will show the mummy's bones, and reveal the amulets hidden in the layers of linen. CAT scans use X-rays that build up a 3-D picture of the mummy's insides. This can show whether the internal organs were removed or how the person died. A mummy's DNA can be extracted by rehydrating its skin. This will help identify who its relatives were. Using a technique called carbon dating, scientists can also estimate the age of a mummy by measuring its carbon levels.

X-rays reveal this mummy's skeleton, and the outline of its coffin.

The pharaohs

THE EGYPTIANS RECORDED events by reference to the year of a king's reign. They did not use dates as we do today. It was a Ptolemaic scholar, Manetho, who sorted the reigns into dynasties using ancient king lists. The dates on this list are all approximate.

Early Dynastic Period (3100–2686 BCE)

1ST DYNASTY (3100–2890 BCE)
Narmer unifies Egypt and Egyptian civilization begins.

Narmer	3100
Aha	3100
Djer	3000
Djet	2980
Den	2950
Anedjib	2925
Semerkhet	2900
Qaa	2890

2ND DYNASTY (2890–2686 BCE)
Monumental stone building of royal tombs begins.

Hetepsekhemwy	2890
Raneb	2865
Nynetjer	
Weneg	
Sened	
Peribsen	2700
Khasekhemwy	2686

First Intermediate Period (2181–2055 BCE)

7TH & 8TH DYNASTIES (2181–2125 BCE)
During this unstable period of ancient Egyptian history there were numerous minor and short-lived kings. We have only sketchy knowledge of their names and deeds. The weakening of centralized power led to the establishment of local dynasties.

9TH & 10TH DYNASTIES (2160–2055 BCE)
Heracleopolitan

Kheti
Merykara
Ity

11th DYNASTY (Thebes Only)

Intef I	2125–2112
Intef II	2112–2063
Intef III	2063–2055

Middle Kingdom (2055–1650 BCE)

11TH DYNASTY (2055–1985 BCE)
Egypt is reunified. Borders are strengthened. Art, culture, and trade flourish.

Mentuhotep I	2055–2004
Mentuhotep II	2004–1992
Mentuhotep III	1992–1985

Limestone statue of Mentuhotep I

12TH DYNASTY (1985–1795 BCE)
Pyramid-building is revived. Public works boost trade and agriculture.

Amenemhat I	1985–1955
Senusret I	1965–1920
Amenemhat II	1922–1878
Senusret II	1880–1874
Senusret III	1874–1855
Amenemhat III	1855–1808
Amenemhat IV	1808–1799
Sobeknefru*	1799–1795

New Kingdom (1550–1069 BCE)

18TH DYNASTY (1550–1295 BCE)
Egypt acquires a Middle Eastern empire. Culture and trade flourish. Period ends in religious upheaval.

Ahmose	1550–1525
Amenhotep I	1525–1504
Thutmose I	1504–1492
Thutmose II	1492–1479
Thutmose III	1479–1425
Hatshepsut*	1473–1458
Amenhotep II	1427–1400
Thutmose IV	1400–1390
Amenhotep III	1390–1352
Akhenaten	1352–1336
Smenkhkare	1338–1336

Tutankhamun	1336–1327
Ay	1327–1323
Horemheb	1323–1295

Gold death mask of Tutankhamun

19TH DYNASTY (1295–1186 BCE)
Strong rule and massive building works. Last truly great dynasty.

Ramesses I	1295–1294
Seti I	1294–1279
Ramesses II	1279–1213
Merneptah	1213–1203
Amenmessu	1203–1200
Seti II	1200–1194
Siptah	1194–1188
Tausret*	1188–1186

Mummy of Ramesses II

20TH DYNASTY (1186–1069 BCE)
Decline of royal power, ending with priests of Amun taking control in the south.

Sethnakhte	1186–1184
Ramesses III	1184–1153
Ramesses IV	1153–1147
Ramesses V	1147–1143
Ramesses VI	1143–1136
Ramesses VII	1136–1129
Ramesses VIII	1129–1126
Ramesses IX	1126–1108
Ramesses X	1108–1099
Ramesses XI	1099–1069

Late Period (747–332 BCE)

26TH DYNASTY (672–525 BCE) (Saite)
Assyrian empire invades Egypt and is pushed out by Psamtek I.

Necho I	672–664
Psamtek I	664–610
Necho II	610–595
Psamtek II	595–589
Apries	589–570
Ahmose II	570–526
Psamtek III	526–525

27TH DYNASTY (525–359 BCE) (Persian Period 1)
Collapse of Assyrian empire leaves power vacuum. Persians invade and form dynasty.

Cambyses	525–522
Darius I	522–486
Xerxes I	486–465
Artaxerxes I	465–424
Darius II	424–405
Artaxerxes II	405–359

28TH DYNASTY (404–c. 380 BCE)
Egyptians regain independence from Persia under Amyrtaeus.

Amyrtaeus	404–399

29TH DYNASTY (399–380 BCE)
Line of native kings.

Nepherites I	399–393
Hakor	393–380
Nepherites II	c. 380

30TH DYNASTY (380–343 BCE)
Persia reinvades. Nectanebo II is last Egyptian king in history.

Nectanebo I	380–362
Teos	362–360
Nectanebo II	360–343

Head of Nectanebo I carved from schist

Old Kingdom (2686–2181 BCE)

3RD DYNASTY (2686–2613 BCE)
The Step Pyramid is built at Saqqara in the reign of Djoser.

Sanakht	2686–2667
Djoser	2667–2648
Sekhemkhet	2648–2640
Khaba	2640–2637
Huni	2637–2613

4TH DYNASTY (2613–2494 BCE)
The pyramids of Giza are built by Khufu, Khafra, and Menkaura.

Sneferu	2613–2589
Khufu	2589–2566
Djedefra	2566–2558
Khafra	2558–2532
Menkaura	2532–2503
Shepseskaf	2503–2494

The pyramids at Giza, built in the 4th Dynasty

5TH DYNASTY (2494–2345 BCE)
The first Sun Temples appear. The Pyramid Texts are written.

Userkaf	2494–2487
Sahur	2487–2475
Neferirkara	2475–2455
Shepseskara	2455–2448
Raneferef	2448–2445
Nyuserra	2445–2421
Menkauhor	2421–2414
Djedkara	2414–2375
Unas	2375–2345

6TH DYNASTY (2345–2181 BCE)
Provincial governors and local nobles become powerful. The pharaoh's rule is weakened.

Teti	2345–2323
Userkara	2323–2321
Pepi I	2321–2287
Merenra	2287–2278
Pepi II	2278–2184
Nitocris*	2184–2181

*denotes female pharaoh

Second Intermediate Period (1650–1550 BCE)

Wooden model of Senusret I

13TH DYNASTY (1795–c. 1725 BCE)
Ten minor kings rule for about 70 years. The history is confused.

14TH DYNASTY (1750–1650 BCE)
Minor kings probably ruling at the same time as the 13th Dynasty.

15TH DYNASTY (1650–1550 BCE)
The Hyksos form a dynasty. First horse and chariot used in war.

Salitis	
Khyan	c. 1600
Apepi	c. 1555
Khamudi	

16TH DYNASTY (1650–1550 BCE)
Minor kings rule parts of Egypt with Hyksos assent.

17TH DYNASTY (1650–1550 BCE)
The kings of Thebes organize campaigns against the Hyksos and expel them from Egypt.

Intef	
Ta I	
Seqenenre Taa II	c. 1560
Kamose	1555–1550

Third Intermediate Period (1069–715 BCE)

21ST DYNASTY (1069–945 BCE)
Pharaohs rule from Tanis in the Delta. Priests rule in the south.

Smendes	1069–1043
Amenemnisu	1043–1039
Psusennes I	1039–991
Amenemope	993–984
Osorkon the Elder	984–978
Siamun	978–959
Psusennes II	959–945

Silver coffin of Psusennes I from Tanis

22ND DYNASTY (945–715 BCE)
Dynasty of Libyan kings established after Libyans rise to prominence in the army.

Sheshonq I	945–924
Osorkon I	924–889
Sheshonq II	c. 890
Takelot I	889–874
Osorkon II	874–850
Takelot II	850–825
Sheshonq III	825–773
Pimay	773–767
Sheshonq V	767–730
Osorkon IV	730–715

23RD DYNASTY (818–715 BCE)
Several continuous lines of rulers at Heracleopolis Magna, Hermopolis Magna, Leontopolis, and Tanis, including the following:

Pedubastis I	818–793
Sheshonq IV	c. 780
Osorkon III	777–749

24TH DYNASTY (727–715 BCE)
Coalition of northern kings attempt to stop growing Nubian influence in the south.

Bakenrenef	727–715

Late Period

25TH DYNASTY (747–656 BCE)
Nubian kings invade Egypt and rule as pharaohs.

Piy	747–716
Shabaqo	716–702
Shabitqo	702–690
Taharqo	690–664
Tanutamani	664–656

Tomb model (shabti) figure of Taharqo

Ptolemaic Period (332–30 BCE)

Persian Period 2 (343–332 BCE)
Persian rule returns to Egypt for II years before being vanquished by Alexander the Great.

Artaxerxes III Ochus	343–338
Arses	338–336
Darius III Codoman	336–332

MACEDONIAN DYNASTY (332–305 BCE)
Alexander the Great is declared pharaoh and divine liberator.

Alexander the Great	332–323
Philip Arrhidaeus	323–317
Alexander IV	317–305

Marble bust of Cleopatra

PTOLEMAIC DYNASTY (305–80 BCE)

Ptolemy I	305–285
Ptolemy II	285–246
Ptolemy III	246–221
Ptolemy IV	221–205
Ptolemy V	205–180
Ptolemy VI	180–145
Ptolemy VII	145
Ptolemy VIII	170–116
Ptolemy IX	116–107
Ptolemy X	107–88
Ptolemy IX	88–80

PTOLEMAIC DYNASTY CONT. (80–30 BCE)
Greek rule over Egypt ends with death of Cleopatra in 30 BCE.

Ptolemy XI	80
Ptolemy XII	80–51
Cleopatra VII*	51–30
Ptolemy XIII	51–47
Ptolemy XIV	47–44
Ptolemy XV	44–30

Egypt becomes part of the Roman empire in 30 BCE.

The gods

OVER THE COURSE OF THEIR 3,000-year history, the ancient Egyptians may have worshiped as many as 2,000 gods. Most gods changed their character and appearance over the centuries, and were popular at different times. Some grew in prestige, while others died out. Here are examples of some of the most important deities.

Ra
Ra, the sun god, represented the sun, and kingship. Eventually, he was joined with Amun to become Amun-Ra, and with Horus to become Ra-Harakhty (*left*).

Khnum
The ram-headed god Khnum presided over the hazardous Nile cataracts. It was on his word that the god Hapy rose to cause the annual flood.

Geb
In one myth, the earth god Geb and his wife, the sky goddess Nut, created the sun, which is reborn each day. A goose is the hieroglyph for Geb's name.

Ptah
Ptah's center of worship was at Memphis. The city's priests maintained that he was the supreme god, who created the other gods by speaking their names.

Anubis
The jackal-headed Anubis was the god of the dead and of mummification. He watched over the embalming process and supervised the numerous different funeral rites.

Nephthys
This goddess helped her sister, Isis, to resurrect Osiris's mutilated body. The sisters are often pictured next to each other on coffins as a pair of hawks.

Sobek
This crocodile god was the ruler of the Nile, which was said to be his sweat. His cult sites grew up in places where the danger of crocodile attacks was high.

Horus   Isis   Osiris

Abydos triad
Triads were families of gods worshiped in certain areas. The Abydos triad were Osiris, the god of the dead, his wife Isis, the goddess of nature and fertility, and their son Horus, the god of the sky, light, and life.

Theban triad
The chief god worshiped at the temple of Karnak at Thebes was the creator god Amun, who was associated with fertility. His wife Mut, a name meaning "mother," was a war goddess, sometimes shown as a vulture. Their son was Khons, a moon god, often shown as a mummy.

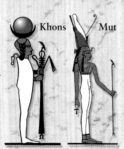

Khons   Mut   Amun

Forms of Maat
Many gods took various forms in different times or settings. Here are three representations of the goddess Maat, who stood for justice, truth, and order. In each, she is wearing the Feather of Truth upon her head.

Seth
Seth was the god of deserts, storms, chaos, and evil. He was associated with animals abhorrent to the Egyptians, including the hippopotamus, the donkey, and the pig.

Hathor
This goddess of the sky, of love, and of happiness was associated with the cow. Hathor was often shown with cow's horns that held the disc of the sun.

Thoth
A patron of scribes and the god of wisdom and writing, Thoth was thought to be the wisest of all. He was also a moon god and was shown as an ibis or as a baboon.

Hieroglyphs

EGYPTIAN WRITING IS called hieroglyphs, a Greek word meaning "sacred symbols." By the Middle Kingdom, scribes were using more than 750 hieroglyphs, of which there were four types. Some stood for sounds, and some for groups of sounds. Others stood for whole words or ideas. The remaining hieroglyphs clarified ambiguity.

EGYPTIAN NUMBERS

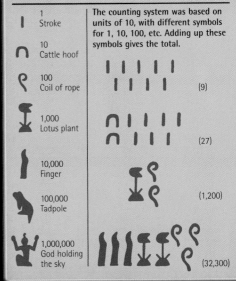

		The counting system was based on units of 10, with different symbols for 1, 10, 100, etc. Adding up these symbols gives the total.
I	1 Stroke	
∩	10 Cattle hoof	(9)
ℙ	100 Coil of rope	(27)
🪷	1,000 Lotus plant	(1,200)
I	10,000 Finger	
🐸	100,000 Tadpole	(32,300)
👤	1,000,000 God holding the sky	

SOUNDS AND SIGNS

The 24 simplest hieroglyphs (shown below) represent single sounds. The Egyptians mainly produced hieroglyphs for consonants, and did not usually include signs for vowels. The pronunciation guide below roughly transliterates these hieroglyphs into something resembling our own alphabet. Writing out a separate sign to represent each sound was time-consuming, so alphabetic hieroglyphs were rarely used in isolation, but with signs that represented combinations of sounds, or whole words.

A as in apple	B as in boy	C as in cent	Ch as in chip
Vulture	Leg	Folded cloth	Tethering rope
D as in dog	F as in far	G as in girl	H as in hat
Hand	Horned viper	Pot stand	Twisted flax
I as in it	J as in jump	K as in kite	L as in lion
Flowering reed	Snake	Basket	Lion
M as in man	N as in new	O as in old	P as in pig
Owl	Water	Lasso	Stool
Q as in queen	R as in rabbit	S as in sit	T as in toy
Hill	Mouth	Folded cloth	Loaf
Th as in that	V as in viper	W as in wig	Z as in zoo
Unknown	Horned viper	Quail chick	Door bolt

Sounds and ideas

Most alphabetic hieroglyphs were combined with "group" signs, standing for more than one sound, or with "idea" signs, which stood for a whole word. We can see how this worked by deciphering this cartouche. The last two signs represent an "S" sound. The central sign stands for the group sound, "MS". The first sign, a sun, is an idea sign and stands for the sun god, "RA." By guessing the missing vowels we get the king's name "RAMESSES."

RA   MS   S S

Special signs

Some hieroglyphs did not represent sounds at all, but were added to clarify meaning. These are called "determinatives." For example, determinatives were used to make it clear who was saying or doing the thing in the sentence. Other signs were thought to have magical properties and were added to counter evil. Like determinatives, they had no sound value.

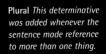

Fighting evil
Scribes sometimes drew snakes with their head cut off. This symbolized an attack on the snake's venom, and would be used on coffins to protect the dead.

Plural *This determinative was added whenever the sentence made reference to more than one thing.*

Man and woman *These determinatives were used at the end of a name, so that the reader could tell whether the subject of the sentence was a man (left) or a woman (right).*

How a mummy is made

The body was washed to symbolize its rebirth into a new life.

Mummy-making

THE EGYPTIANS BELIEVED that a person's spirit would search for its body after death and revisit it in the tomb. The person's body therefore had to be preserved as a mummy, so that the spirit would always have a home. The mummy also had to look lifelike, so that the spirit would recognize its old self.

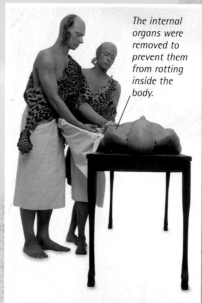

The internal organs were removed to prevent them from rotting inside the body.

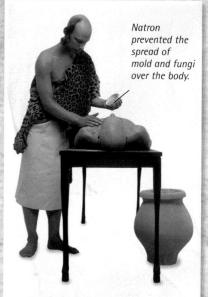

Natron prevented the spread of mold and fungi over the body.

1. WASHING
The body was first taken to the *ibu* (purification place), where it was washed and cleaned. The water contained a salty mineral called natron, which dried the skin and killed bacteria. Washing took place as soon as possible after death in order to begin the preservation process.

2. REMOVING THE ORGANS
Embalmers then moved the body into the *wabt* (mummifying tent), and removed the brain. After that, the internal organs were pulled out through a neat slit made in the side of the body. These were then mummified separately.

3. SALTING THE CORPSE
The corpse was then an empty shell ready to be dried out. The embalmers filled the body cavity with natron in order to remove moisture and to dissolve body fat. They then covered the corpse with a large pile of natron and left it to dry for 40 days.

Duamutef, a jackal, guarded the stomach.

Qebehsenuef, a falcon, guarded the intestines.

Hapy, a baboon, guarded the lungs.

Imsety, a man, guarded the liver.

Storing the internal organs
The embalmers stored the body's internal organs in containers called canopic jars. At the top of each was a stopper, which was carved in the shape of a human or an animal god. These gods, and the spells carved on the jars, gave magical protection to the organ inside. The heart was left inside the body, because the dead person would need it when he or she was judged by the gods.

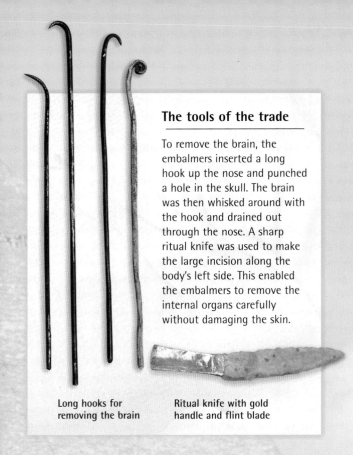

The tools of the trade

To remove the brain, the embalmers inserted a long hook up the nose and punched a hole in the skull. The brain was then whisked around with the hook and drained out through the nose. A sharp ritual knife was used to make the large incision along the body's left side. This enabled the embalmers to remove the internal organs carefully without damaging the skin.

Long hooks for removing the brain

Ritual knife with gold handle and flint blade

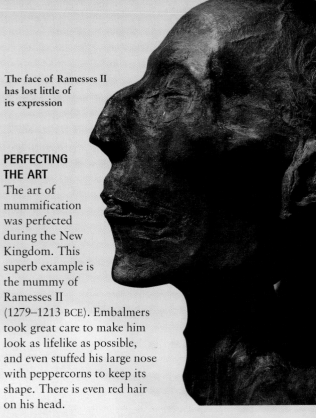

The face of Ramesses II has lost little of its expression

PERFECTING THE ART

The art of mummification was perfected during the New Kingdom. This superb example is the mummy of Ramesses II (1279–1213 BCE). Embalmers took great care to make him look as lifelike as possible, and even stuffed his large nose with peppercorns to keep its shape. There is even red hair on his head.

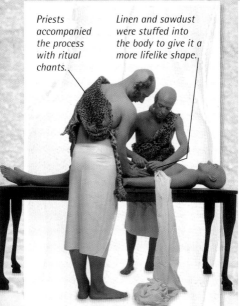

Priests accompanied the process with ritual chants.

Linen and sawdust were stuffed into the body to give it a more lifelike shape.

4. THE NATURAL LOOK

After 40 days, the corpse was dry, blotchy, and stick-thin. The skin was then rubbed with oils to make it supple again. Balls of linen were inserted into the eye sockets and the eyelids pulled down to create a sleeping appearance. The slit in the body's side was sealed.

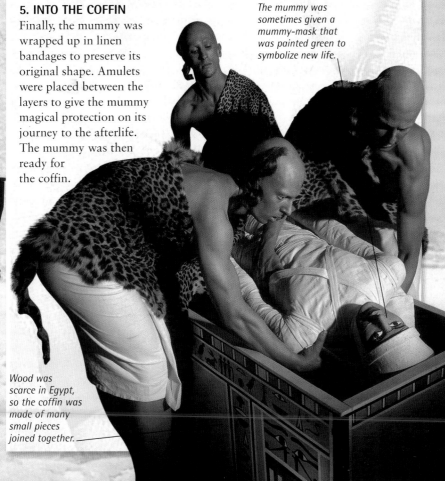

5. INTO THE COFFIN

Finally, the mummy was wrapped up in linen bandages to preserve its original shape. Amulets were placed between the layers to give the mummy magical protection on its journey to the afterlife. The mummy was then ready for the coffin.

The mummy was sometimes given a mummy-mask that was painted green to symbolize new life.

Wood was scarce in Egypt, so the coffin was made of many small pieces joined together.

Glossary

Words in *italics* have their own entry in the glossary.

A

Abydos Ancient burial site in the middle part of Egypt where the kings of the early *Dynasties* were buried.

Amarna Modern name for Akhetaten, the capital city built by *New Kingdom pharaoh* Akhenaten (1352–1336 BCE) in the middle part of Egypt.

amulet Object worn as a protective device or lucky charm to ward off evil.

ankh *Hieroglyph* for the word meaning "life," shaped like a cross with a looped head.

Atef crown Tall, feathered crown worn by *pharaohs* on state occasions.

B

ba A person's spirit or soul, thought to live on after death. The *ba* was often shown as a bird with a human head.

barque In ancient Egypt, a Nile boat and also the boat used by the sun god, Ra, to sail across the heavens.

ben–ben stone Sacred *pyramid*-shaped stone worshiped at Heliopolis and thought to be the original *Mound of Creation*.

Blue Crown Large, bulb-shaped war crown worn by the *pharaohs* of the *New Kingdom*.

Book of the Dead Collection of about 200 spells, placed with the *mummy* as protection during the journey to the afterlife.

C

canopic jars Four jars that held the mummified stomach, liver, lungs, and intestines of a dead person.

cartonnage Material made from linen stiffened with plaster, and used to make mummy-masks and coffins.

cartouche Oval drawn around the name of the ruler. The shape symbolized eternity and put the ruler under the magical protection of the gods.

cataract Place where the Nile passes rapidly between granite rocks. The first cataract marked the border between Egypt and *Nubia*; other cataracts were farther south.

co–regency System of rule established in the *Middle Kingdom* whereby an appointed successor ruled alongside the *pharaoh* to ensure stability after the pharaoh's death.

crook Staff used to tend sheep. In ancient Egypt, the *pharaoh* held a crook in his right hand as a symbol of his kingship. In his left hand he held the *flail*.

D

Dahshur *Pyramid* site situated to the south of *Memphis* and used by the rulers of the 4th and 12th *Dynasties*.

Deir el–Bahri Site near the *Valley of the Kings* of large temples built by Mentuhotep I (11th Dynasty) and Queen Hatshepsut (18th Dynasty)

Deir el–Medina Village close to the *Valley of the Kings* where the valley's tomb workers were housed.

Delta Fertile area of *Lower Egypt* where the Nile fans out into many branches before reaching the Mediterranean Sea.

demotic Shorthand style of handwriting that developed from the *hieratic* script.

Deshret Ancient Egyptian name for the desert, meaning "Red Land," after the color of the sand.

djed pillar *Hieroglyph* for the word meaning "stability." Its shape was a representation of the backbone of Osiris.

Double Crown A combination of the *White Crown* and the *Red Crown*, and worn by the *pharaoh* to symbolize his kingship over *Upper* and *Lower Egypt*.

dynasty Series of *pharaohs* from related families. Egypt's native *pharaohs* formed 30 dynasties.

E

Early Dynastic Period Period of Egyptian history when the 1st *Dynasty* rulers emerged. It lasted until the end of the 2nd *Dynasty* (3100–2686 BCE).

emmer Type of wheat common in ancient Egypt.

equinox The two days in each year when the hours of day and night are of equal length.

F

faience Material formed from a paste of crushed quartz. It was fired hard in a kiln and glazed, and used to make small objects such as *amulets*.

First Intermediate Period Period of Egyptian history from the beginning of 7th to the end of the 10th *Dynasties* of rulers (2181–2055 BCE). Between the *Old* and *Middle Kingdoms*.

flail An agricultural tool used to cut wheat. Held by the king in his left hand as a symbol of the fertility of the land. In his right hand he held a *crook*.

G

Giza Site near modern Cairo of the largest Egyptian *pyramids*, which were built by the *Old Kingdom* pharaohs Khufu, Khafra, and Menkaura.

grave goods Items such as food, clothes, and jewelry that were buried with the *mummy* for use in the afterlife.

H

Hawara *Middle Kingdom pyramid* site in *Lower Egypt*, south of *Giza*.

Heracleopolis Capital city of ancient Egypt during the *First Intermediate Period*.

Hieraconpolis Earliest capital city of Egypt, before the time of the 1st *Dynasty* and situated to the south of *Thebes*. Its name means "Falcon City" after the falcon-headed god, Horus.

hieratic

hieratic Form of handwriting that developed from *hieroglyphs* and was quicker to write.

hieroglyphs The oldest writing script used in ancient Egypt, consisting of picture signs that refer to the meaning and sound of words.

Hyksos Group of foreigners who settled in Egypt from Palestine and formed the 15th *Dynasty* of rulers. They introduced new elements into Egyptian warfare, such as the horse and chariot.

hypostyle Style of hall built during the *New Kingdom*. Hypostyle halls had many large stone columns. From a Greek word meaning "resting on pillars."

I

ibis A river bird with a long, thin beak, thought to be the embodiment of Thoth, the god of knowledge and writing. Thoth was portrayed with the head of an ibis.

inundation Period between June and September when the Nile flooded each year.

J K

ka Life force or "double" of a living person, formed at birth. After death, the *ka* survived in the dead person's tomb, provided there were offerings left there for it.

Karnak Vast temple complex at Thebes dedicated to the god Amun-Ra. Karnak was at its largest extent during the *New Kingdom*.

Kemet Ancient Egyptian name for Egypt meaning "Black Land," after the color of the mud deposited by the Nile when it flooded.

L

Lapis lazuli Highly prized dark blue stone from Afghanistan, used in ancient Egypt for *amulets* and jewelry.

Late Period Period of Egyptian history from the beginning of the 25th *Dynasty* to the end of the Persian period (747–332 BCE).

Libya The desert lands to the west of Egypt.

Lisht *Pyramid* site in *Lower Egypt* south of *Dahshur*, where 12th *Dynasty* rulers were buried.

lotus flower Flower used for making perfume. Also the emblem of *Upper Egypt*.

Lower Egypt The northern region of ancient Egypt.

M

mastaba Rectangular bench-shaped tomb with a flat roof.

Memphis Capital city of Egypt during the *Old Kingdom*. Situated south of the Nile *Delta*.

Middle Kingdom Period of Egyptian history from the beginning of the 11th to the end of the 14th *Dynasties* of rulers (2055–1650 BCE).

Mound of Creation Island thought to have arisen from the waters of chaos at the moment of the creation of the world.

mummy Preserved body. In ancient Egypt, human and animal bodies were artificially mummified by being dried out with *natron*, then wrapped with linen bandages.

N

Naqada culture Name given to the people who settled in the Nile Valley in the time before the *Early Dynastic Period*.

Narmer Palette Stone plate found at *Hieraconpolis*, and carved with images that celebrate the conquest of *Lower Egypt* by Narmer, a king of *Upper Egypt*.

natron Type of salt found on the shores of lakes in Egypt. Natron was used to dry bodies during the process of mummification.

nemes headdress Striped cloth worn as a headdress by the *pharaoh*.

New Kingdom Period of Egyptian history from the beginning of the 18th to the end of the 20th *Dynasties* of rulers (1550–1069 BCE).

nilometer Type of well that connected to the Nile. Using a scale marked on its wall, Egyptians monitored the river's level during the annual flood.

nome Name given to an administrative district of ancient Egypt.

Nubia Country to the south of Egypt, exploited by Egypt for gold, stone and slaves.

O

obelisk Tall stone with a *pyramid*-shaped top used to commemorate royal deeds.

Old Kingdom Period of Egyptian history from the beginning of the 3rd to the end of the 6th *Dynasties* of rulers (2686–2181 BCE).

Opening of the Mouth Ceremony performed on *mummies* so that their senses would be reborn in the afterlife.

P

papyrus Water reed used to make writing paper, baskets, ropes, sandals, and medicine. Also the emblem of *Lower Egypt*.

pharaoh King or queen of ancient Egypt.

pylon Large stone gateway marking the entrance to a temple. From a Greek word meaning "gate."

pyramid Tomb with a square base and four sloping sides, built to hold the mummified body of a *pharaoh*.

Pyramid Texts Collections of religious hymns and spells found in the *pyramids* of the *Old Kingdom*.

Q R

Red Crown Crown worn by rulers to symbolize their authority over *Lower Egypt*.

regent A person who governs the country when the rightful ruler is too young or too old to govern. In ancient Egypt, the *pharaoh*'s mother sometimes ruled until he was old enough.

relief Sculpture carved on a flat surface. Figures carved on the surface could be raised or sunken.

ritual beard Triangular, artificial beard worn by the ruler during royal ceremonies.

Rosetta Stone Stone slab discovered in 1799 on which was carved the same message in *hieroglyphs*, *demotic*, and Greek. The stone was invaluable in helping to decode hieroglyphs, since scholars could compare the same royal names in each script.

S

saff tomb Type of tomb built for the rulers of the early 11th *Dynasty*. Saff tombs were cut into rock with a row of pillars at the entrance. The name comes from the Arabic word for "row."

Saqqara Burial ground near *Memphis*, south of Cairo, used for royal and private burials.

sarcophagus Stone coffin. The word is from the Greek for "flesh-eater."

satrap Persian term for a subordinate provincial ruler.

scarab Type of beetle considered sacred by the ancient Egyptians.

scimitar Sword with a broad, curved blade that was introduced to Egypt from Syria during the 18th *Dynasty*.

scribe Person trained to read, write, and calculate figures.

Second Intermediate Period Period of Egyptian history from the beginning of the 15th to the end of the 17th *Dynasty* of rulers (1650–1550 BCE). Between the *Middle* and *New Kingdoms*.

sed festival Festival for symbolically renewing a *pharaoh*'s divine strength, held in the 30th year of his reign.

senet Board game similar to today's game of checkers, played on a board of 30 squares.

serdab Sealed chamber within a tomb usually containing a statue of the dead person. From the Arabic word for "cellar."

serekh Rectangular frame drawn around the name of a ruler. Used during the *Old Kingdom* and in *Early Dynastic Period*.

shabtis Small statues placed in a tomb. Shabtis were thought to come alive in the afterlife to act as servants for the dead.

sidelock of youth Long lock of hair worn by children. A boy's lock was ritually cut off when he became an adult.

sphinx Creature with a lion's body and human head, particularly that of the *pharaoh*.

stela Large, rectangular block of stone covered in symbols and *hieroglyphs*.

T

Thebes Capital of Egypt during the *New Kingdom*.

Third Intermediate Period Period of Egyptian history from the beginning of the 21st to the end of the 24th *Dynasties* of rulers (1069–715 BCE). Between the *New Kingdom* and the *Late Period*.

U

Upper Egypt The southern region of ancient Egypt.

V

Valley of the Kings Burial site in the desert to the west of *Thebes*, used during the *New Kingdom* for the burial of *pharaoh*s in rock-cut tombs.

Vizier The chief minister and the highest official in the government. He kept the pharaoh informed on all matters.

W X Y Z

Weighing of the heart A trial in which the god Anubis weighed a dead person's heart against the Feather of Truth, to see if the person was worthy of entering the afterlife.

White Crown Tall, pawn-shaped crown worn by rulers to symbolize their authority over *Upper Egypt*.

Index

Credits

Dorling Kindersley would like to thank:
Chris Bernstein for the index; Rosie O'Neill and Kate Bradshaw for editorial assistance; and Mark Millmore of Eyelid Productions for his digital illustrations.

The publisher would like to thank the following for their kind permission to reproduce their photographs:
(Abbreviations key: t=top, b=bottom, r=right, l=left, c=center)

akg-images: 57c, 130l; Andrea Jemolo 6-7cb, 13tr, 13br, 34tl, 48cbl, 94l, 95c, 114tl; Erich Lessing 10l, 16tl, 24tl, 31tr, 49b, 53br, 72-73t, 81r, 88l, 105br, 109r, 115t, 126t, 128-129bc; Francois Guénet 108tl; Francois Guénet/Egyptian Museum, Cairo 101r; Robert O'Dea 68-69t; The Egyptian Museum, Cairo 43br, 136c. Alamy Images: Peter Bowater 142-143, 144; Sylvain Grandadam/Robert Harding Picture Library 127, 129r. Ancient Art & Architecture Collection: 100bc, 100t, 106-107cb, 113tl; J. Stevens 23tl; R. Sheridan 78-79b, 100bl. The Ancient Egypt Picture Library: 21tr, 22br, 22l, 23br, 27br, 41tr, 46cb, 47c, 51br, 56-57, 61tr, 63br, 71br,

81b, 101tl; Cairo Museum 49r, 137cla; Luxor Museum 3bcll, 77cbl, 80tl. The Art Archive: Archaeological Museum Naples/Dagli Orti 134tl; Bibliotheque des Arts Decoratifs Paris/Dagli Orti 88tr; British Museum/Dagli Orti 41br; Dagli Orti 12tl, 32-33cbs, 37tr, 44cbr, 45clb, 50-51, 52bl, 102-103, 108-109c, 110bl, 121clb, 122-123, 123tr, 128c; Egyptian Museum Cairo/Dagli Orti 25cb, 44-45, 84b, 95clb, 102bc, 104tl; 107clb, 113cr, 120crb, 122l, 123br, 136cbr, 141tr; Egyptian Museum of Cairo 103r; Musée du Louvre Paris/Dagli Orti 22bc, 40bl, 96tl, 104cl, 104clb, 106crb, 108bl, 140bl; Museo della Civiltà Romana Rome/Dagli Orti 130bc; Museo Nazionale Romano Rome/Dagli Orti 129cr; Ragab Papyrus Institute Cairo/Dagli Orti 89br. Art Directors & TRIP: 110tl; H Rogers 110-111c. Charles Best: 28-29, 54, 66-67bs, 70, 74bl, 95r, 112bcr, 116b, 118-119, 140cl, 140c, 140cr, 141bl, 141br. Photo Courtesy of Jon Bodsworth, The Egypt Archive: The Egyptian Museum, Cairo Archive 20tl. www.bridgeman.co.uk: Ashmolean Museum, University of Oxford 95cb, 96bl; Brooklyn Museum of Art, New York, USA 47br; Brooklyn Museum of Art, New York/Charles Edwin Wilbour Fund 36tl; Egyptian National Museum, Cairo 3bcr, 90, 98tl, 100cb; Egyptian National Museum, Cairo/Giraudon 91clb, 98-99; Egyptian National Museum, Cairo, Egypt 136cbl; Peter Willi/Louvre, Paris, France

14bl; Peter Willi/Musee des Beaux Arts, Grenoble, France 126bl. Peter Clayton: 46-47. Corbis: 4-5t, 19clb, 30-31; Archivo Iconografico, S.A 64tl, 67br, 75tl, 79tr, 90crb, 90-91cb, 92l, 97r; Bob Rowan; Progressive Image 40l; Charles & Josette Lenars 105tc; Charles O'Rear 67tr; Christine Osborne 82bl; Craig Tuttle 64-65t; Gary Braasch 130-131tr; Gian Berto Vanni 3bcr, 106; Gianni Dagli Orti 36-37, 41bc, 62l, 72cl, 96-97, 115br, 123cr, 125tr; Giraud Philippe/Sygma 2bcr, 6; Jonathan Blair 120-121cb, 124-125c, 124-125t; K.M Westermann 62-63, 63tl; Larry Lee Photography 140-141; M. Angelo 138; Martin B. Withers; Frank Lane Picture Agency 6cbr, 8-9b; Michael Nicholson 68-69b, 70tl, 78bl; Mike Southern; Eye Ubiquitous 87t; O. Alamany & E. Vicens 76cbr, 85br; Patrick Bennett 114-115t; Paul Almasy 56tl, 111; Pierre Vauthey/Sygma 8-9t; Randy Faris 2br, 18-19; Richard T. Nowitz 93r; Robert Holmes 14-15c; Roger Wood 17tl, 34tr, 75br, 116t, 118tr, 132-133, 137clb; Ron Watts 3bl, 32-33; Ruggero Vanni 94tr; Sandro Vannini 71tr, 84t, 103bc, 112, 130bcr, 134bc, 137bc; Vanni Archive 54-55t; Werner Forman 15r; Wolfgang Kaehler 66tc. DK Images: British Museum 3br, 14br, 16bl, 16br, 38-39b, 46cl, 48l, 48t, 53t, 55tr, 55br, 56bl, 58-59cb, 60tl, 63tr, 63crb, 64cl, 64b, 65b, 65r, 75tc, 75cra, 75bcr, 78tl, 83br, 88br, 88-89, 89tr, 100 (linen), 124ca, 125br,

135tl, 137crb, 141ca; Copyright Judith Miller/DK- Sloan's USA 14crb; Daniel Moignot, P.L.J. Gallimard Jeunesse Larousse 28clb; Rosicrucian Egyptian Museum, San Jose, California 20-21; Stephen Hayward 11bc. Matthew Davey: 2-3. Egypt Exploration Society, London: 134-135 (background of boxes). Werner Forman Archive: The Egyptian Museum, Cairo 33cbl, 39r. Getty Images: Kathleen Campbell 1; Michael McQueen 3bcl, 58; Rosemary Calvert 4-5c. Griffith Institute, Oxford: 42-43; Harry Burton 101tcl. Robert Harding Picture Library: F.L. Kenett 99tr; Rainbird 98-99. © Michael Holford: 3bc, 76. Model Designed: Barry Kemp, Michael Mallinson and Kate Spence. Built by Andrew Ingham Associates, Photography by David Grandorge: 93tl. Jurgen Liepe: 58cbr, 59cbl, 60bl, 72-73b. Mark Millmore/Eyelid Productions: 3br, 12, 18-19c, 26-27, 32cbr, 34-35, 76-77cb, 86, 120-121. NASA: 52tr. National Geographic Image Collection: Kenneth Garrett 82-83, 87br. Petrie Museum of Egyptian Archaeology, University College London: 57br. Reuters: Aladin Abdel Naby 117t. Science & Society Picture Library: Science Museum 141tl. Science Photo Library: Brian Brake 7cbl, 16-17, 136-137; John Sanford 26tc, 42-43tr, 52-53tr, 66-67t; NASA 11. Topfoto.co.uk: The British Museum/HIP 128t, 136br.